/ 75

CHRISTIAN VOCATION
Studies in Faith and Work

First published 1951

To
MY FATHER
and
MY MOTHER

Printed in Great Britain by
Latimer, Trend & Co. Ltd., Plymouth

CHRISTIAN VOCATION

STUDIES IN FAITH AND WORK

being the Cunningham Lectures, 1950
in New College, Edinburgh

by

W. R. FORRESTER

Professor of Christian Ethics and Practical Theology
St. Mary's College, University of St. Andrews

LUTTERWORTH PRESS
LONDON

AUTHOR'S ACKNOWLEDGMENTS

I acknowledge gratefully permission to use material from Principal R. Newton Flew's book, *The Idea of Perfection*, quoted on pp. 47-8, from the author and from the Clarendon Press, Oxford; from the Oxford University Press for the quotations from Edwyn Bevan's *Christianity* in the Home University Library on pp. 45-7; from Messrs. Hodder and Stoughton and the author for the quotation from Dr. William Neil's *Commentary on Thessalonians*, in Moffatt's New Testament Commentaries, on p. 136; from Messrs. Faber and Faber and the author for the quotation from *The Idea of a Christian Society*, by T. S. Eliot, on pp. 211-12; from Messrs. Macmillan and Company and Mrs. Temple for the quotation from *Nature, Man and God*, by Archbishop William Temple, on p. 213; from Messrs Sheed and Ward for the quotation from Borne and Henry, *A Philosophy of Work*, on pp. 165-6; from Messrs. James Nisbet and Company and the author for the quotation from Professor Emil Brunner, *Christianity and Civilisation*, Vol. II, quoted on pp. 154-5; from Messrs. George Allen and Unwin for the quotations from Ernst Troeltsch, *The Social Teaching of the Christian Churches*, on pp. 54-6, and from Max Weber, *The Protestant Ethic*, on p. 154; from the S.P.C.K. for permission to quote from *Theology*, November 1949, on pp. 204-5 and from Ferrar's *Demonstratio Evangelica* of Eusebius, on pp. 42-3; and from Jonathan Cape for permission to quote Arthur Koestler, *The Yogi and the Commissar*, on pp. 178-9. Portions of Chapter 13 appeared in *The Expository Times* for September 1937, and I gratefully acknowledge permission to use this material.

Most of Part Two of this book was given as the Cunningham Lectures in New College, Edinburgh, in January 1950, and to he Trustees of this lectureship I wish to express my cordial thanks. In the preparation of the book I have received much help, and wish to thank especially my colleagues in the Faculty of Divinity and Principal John Baillie of New College, Edinburgh, to whom I am indebted for the reference to Edwyn Bevan on pp. 45-7. To the Staff of my old college, New College, Edinburgh, and to its Librarian, I owe much, as to the Librarians and Staff of the St. Andrews' University Library. The proofs have been read with great care by my father, Rev. D. M. Forrester, D.D., and my friend Mr. W. L. Lorimer, Reader in Latin in this University. I owe much in the preparation of the Index and other matters to my wife, and to the skilful typing of Miss Marjory MacTier and Miss Maude Joyner.

W. R. FORRESTER

St. Mary's College, St. Andrews,
June 8, 1951.

CONTENTS

THE climate of our time is peculiarly inhospitable to the life of the spirit. For one thing we now live in an age of speed where our souls have no opportunity to catch up on our bodies, and revolutionary and breathless change gives us no time to plan the direction in which we ought to move or to formulate the purposes our new skills and gadgets should serve.

The intellectual climate makes faith difficult. We live in an age of relativity where there are no longer any absolutes, and without absolutes the soul cannot live. In *physics* Einstein is only one of many thinkers who have established the reign of relativity and the contingency of many supposed absolute laws of nature. In *biology* Darwin stands for the triumph of the category of evolution over all former static conceptions. In *economics* Marx is supposed to have reduced all our patterns of behaviour to terms of economic pressures and class conflicts, with the result that all our social structures, political, ecclesiastical, and cultural, are supposed to be determined by their economic foundations, or lack of them. Last of all, and from the spiritual point of view worst of all, in *psychology* Freud has uncovered the somewhat crude origins and affiliations of our noblest aspirations. It is in vain that scientists themselves point to the limitation of the scope of evolution, strictly so-called, to the biological sphere, and its application only by analogy to distinctively human affairs and to the realm of inanimate nature. The man in the street has come to believe that in all these spheres the absolute is an anachronism, and that the imponderable is unreal,

7

because the successive spheres of our material world have, one after the other, submitted to measurement, analysis and control, and since the outworks of the soul, in its "psycho-somatic" unity with the body, have been invaded by psychology, many are apprehensive that the scientist may at last penetrate to the holy of holies, and like Titus, on entering and profaning the Temple at Jerusalem, find no one there.

Before 1914 for a man to be called an idealist was a compliment; now, thanks to Marx and Freud, it is a reproach, and means that he is building castles in Spain and is a prey to illusions.

Not only does the prevailing relativity of intellectual theories in the present stage of scientific thought make faith difficult, in practical affairs our obsession with skills and gadgets is itself a hindrance to the reverent attitude of mind in faith and worship. The commonest form of idolatry to-day is the worship of the things we have made with our own hands, and never in recorded history have we had so wide a range of idols to choose from and become absorbed in. It is not merely that we are obsessed with our own techniques, but we have become so accustomed to and dominated by the various mechanisms of our daily work, our educational systems, and our amusements, that we have developed the "mass-mind" which can be manipulated by propaganda and is no longer capable of the responsibilities of citizenship. The putty-like quality of the minds of multitudes of our over-industrialized populations is a sinister and alarming thing. When we remember how the generation that was reared in the earliest phases of compulsory education made the "yellow press" style of journalism possible and inevitable; how subsequent generations, subjected also to the subtle mind-conditioning of the cinema and radio, can in many cases make no higher use of their "education" than to fill in the football pool coupons, we contemplate the future with misgiving. The "mass-mind" is not merely a problem of inertia, it is a volcanic possibility of demonic evil on a portentous scale.

This is not a picture of our age, seen with a somewhat jaundiced eye, nor is it a description of the real contribution to knowledge of the great thinkers mentioned, but it is an impressionistic attempt to draw attention to certain dangers threatening our age, so that the more effective our scientific knowledge and educational and other techniques become, the greater also the danger to our spiritual values becomes.

Our age has now several examples before it, of contemporary urgency, in which we have seen apparently moribund and apathetic multitudes galvanized into startling, violent, purposeful, concerted activity on a heroic level, at the bidding of a "Man of Destiny", who succeeded in convincing them individually that their lives could become worth-while, and that their nation could regain its sense of vocation and shake off its apathy. Germany seemed to experience a genuine rebirth under Hitler and Italy under Mussolini, and a new phase in the strange history of Russia began with Lenin's coming to power. We realize now that *the mass-mind is the raw material out of which the Titans have hammered their powerful weapons.* And yet have we any right to say that what has happened to leaders and peoples in Italy, Germany and Russia is "Titanism", while what happened here in 1940 and through the war years under Churchill was due to a real sense of vocation? What, after all, is this sense of vocation, and how does it differ from ruthless ambition in an individual, and lawless nationalism and imperialism in a people? Does the difference lie purely in the character of the national hero? Or in the character of the people he may lead or exploit? Or may it not be some subtle qualities of character or of culture in both leader and people, that strangely unite in a supreme crisis to achieve moral greatness of a heroic stature? It is difficult to imagine a mentality like the German, whose political incompetence seems satisfied only when it has created a government too strong for its people's liberties and for its neighbours' peace, responding to the leadership of a lover of liberty like Winston Churchill. It is possible that

9

only in war was his sense of vocation confirmed by the loyalty of the people, because it came into its own only in the stresses and opportunities of war. There, too, we have another problem in vocation, for too many people only escaped from meaningless drudgery and insignificant lives under stress of danger in war. Can the sense of purpose which so many discovered in the emergencies and dangers of war-time patriotism be transformed into the duties of peace-time citizenship? The sad experience of disenchantment that has faced two successive generations, after they have each in turn won their war, and the vision of what can be done for better or for worse when a man feels himself to be the man of destiny and persuades a people that it too has a mission in the world—these surely compel us to examine more closely what we mean by "vocation".

Further, we have had poignant experience in the periods of unemployment of the devastating effects upon character of enforced idleness and also of the effects of long-continued, monotonous, mechanical drudgery, especially when this is associated with highly-specialized machinery, so that the worker loses all sense of the wholeness of the "end-product" of the processes that alone immediately concern him, and feels himself to be nothing better than a cog in the machine.

The trouble in industry, we begin to suspect, is much more deep-seated than certain perversions and abuses of a capitalist system. In our towns all sense of neighbourhood and community may be lost and conditions of work and conditions of living conspire to produce a spiritual loneliness and sense of insecurity in social and economic atoms, whose lives and work have ceased to have any real relation to one another or significance for any social and spiritual purposes. Hence comes the disintegration of character and community life, paralleled only by the disintegration of our academic curricula. It is no wonder that under communist or "catholic" inspiration, men frequently thrust themselves into some form of collectivism, or a "catholicism of despair".

In Great Britain we have in recent years embarked on certain social experiments of the utmost importance, the effects of which cannot meantime be foreseen. We are building the Welfare State, to guarantee social security to everyone, and to arrest the deterioration of character and disintegration of community life, too common under *laissez-faire* conditions. The pressure of the primary motives of hunger and fear is relaxed; will this result in a slackening of moral and economic activity? Our standards and values are being changed partly deliberately, partly unconsciously. If the "profit-motive" is deposed from its primacy in our economic life, is the "service motive" itself strong, adequate and flexible enough to provide a substitute for it? Or does the "service motive" require the "vocation-motive" of a sense of religious responsibility as the "end-motive" to give it direction and drive? If so, how is all this to be related to the "adequate incentive" which is the new disguise of the profit-motive? Should we countenance the growth of a new hierarchy of power and privilege to take the place of the profit-motive? Social security can only become a workable policy as well as an ideal if there is a strong sense of corporate responsibility widespread among the people. Otherwise we *may* depose the profit-motive, only to release and exalt in its place a power-motive far more anti-social and morally dangerous. Such a new hierarchy of rewards and privileges need not necessarily be any more Christian than the present capital-labour set-up, or the feudal structure either for that matter. It is a valuable ethical principle that privilege should be related to social function. But who is to assess the value and importance of social function? And what spiritual purpose do those social functions ultimately secure?

The Churches are awakening to the necessity for examination of these and similar questions. The Amsterdam and Lambeth Reports mention "vocation" in one meaning or other of the word in almost every section.

Is there a master-plan for the world, formerly described

as Providence? and how does it operate upon and among the real events of our world? This plan, if it is to be truly spiritual and distinctively Christian, cannot be expressed in any but personal terms, and that brings us back to "vocation".

Has the Church a mission or vocation to the world? In what sense does the Call of God express itself and become embodied in a Calling? In what sense is the "Call" to the ministry to be distinguished from the Call to serve God in a secular employment? In short, what is the true solution for our time of the perennial problem of the relation of the sacred to the secular? But it is time we tried to define what we mean by vocation.

PART ONE

THE CALL

MAINLY THEOLOGICAL

Chapter One

THE MEANING OF VOCATION

VOCATION has been described as "one of the lordliest of words" (W. M. Macgregor), and as "the supreme category of religion" (J. A. Robertson); but no word is more frequently misunderstood, or more frequently misused. The words "vocation", "call", and "calling" are fully described in the New English Dictionary. From the various shades of meaning given to "vocation" there we may without unfairness select three as representing the main important uses of the word:

(1) The action on the part of God (or Christ) of calling persons or mankind into a state of salvation or union with Himself; the fact or condition of being so called.

(2) The action on the part of God in calling a person to exercise some special function, especially of a spiritual nature; or to fill a special position; divine influence or guidance or guidance towards a definite (especially religious) career; the fact of being so called or directed towards a special work in life; natural tendency to, or fitness for, such work.

(3) The particular function or station to which a person is called of God; a mode of life or sphere of action regarded as so determined.

In this special use of (3) we find "vocation" used of one's ordinary occupation, business, or profession.

Those interested in the history and meaning of words should turn up the dictionary on "avocation", where they will find how careless use has led to the degeneration of a word. An "avocation" was originally something that took

15

you away from your real "vocation", a distraction or amuse-
ment. If your course of life was a religious vocation which
involved withdrawal from the world, all secular occupations
and amusements became "avocations" (e.g. Fuller, "Heaven
is his vocation and therefore he counts earthly employments
avocations"). We shall see how important this view is when
we discuss (3) above later on. But a thing which takes your
mind away from something else is probably more interesting
or important than the other thing. So an "avocation" came
to usurp the place of a "vocation", and ultimately the two
words came to be used as if they were interchangeable. An
"avocation of them from their Church employment" (i.e.
something which distracts them from their "heavenly calling") became easily a "sudden avocation to business".[1]

To add to the confusion we have the quite modern use, or
misuse, of "avocation"; as "the Gospel is in the first instance
a call *away* from absorption in the interests, cares and
pleasures of the immediate world" (J. H. Oldham, *Work in
Modern Society*, p. 43), we can get "Baptist and Methodist
preachers often were able to earn part of their living in other
pursuits and to follow the ministry as an avocation" (Pope,
Millhands and Preachers, p. 110), and "all that virile vitality
. . . now poured itself with irresistible force into the avocation of an Evangelical minister" (of John Newton, Lord
David Cecil, in *The Stricken Deer*, p. 118). The original
relationships between "vocation" and "avocation" have here
been exactly reversed.[2]

In current use "vocation" means merely a career. Who was
the agent inspired by the Evil One to apply the word "career"

[1] Perhaps the best illustration of the abuse of the word "vocation" is in
Shakespeare, *Henry IV*, Part I, Act 1, Scene 2, where Falstaff says "Why, Hal,
'tis my vocation, Hal; 'tis no sin for a man to labour in his vocation." Here
the "vocation" is purse-taking! Perhaps it was this reference that induced
Sydney Smith to write of "the ancient avocation of picking pockets".
[2] Note the important contrast made in this passage—"Biological facts have
determined motherhood to be a more absorbing vocation than the avocation
of fatherhood, and thereby inhibited a mother's freedom in developing certain talents which are irrelevant to the maternal function." (Reinhold Niebuhr,
An Interpretation of Christian Ethics, p. 163.)

16

to human affairs? It is a word incapable of redemption, better *Career*
fitted to describe the motion of a horse than the motive of a
man. It is a positive centaur among words and partakes, like
all such hybrids, of the most ignoble qualities of both sides
of its mixed ancestry. How much better is a man than a
mule? Incidentally, all instances of this word used in this
sense given in the N.E.D. date from the nineteenth century.
Was it only with the Industrial Revolution that men started
having "careers"?

"This idea of vocation 'the calling' ", says Brunner,[1] "has
no more than the name in common with that which is called
so to-day. The idea of the Calling has been degraded, so dis-
gracefully, into something quite trivial, it has been denuded
of its daring and liberating religious meaning to such an
extent, and has been made so ordinary and commonplace
that we might even ask whether it would not be better to
renounce it altogether. On the other hand, it is a conception
which in its Scriptural sense is so full of force and so preg-
nant in meaning, it gathers up so clearly the final meaning of
God's acts of grace—the Calling—and the concrete character of the Divine Command in view of the world in which
man has to act, that to renounce this expression would mean
losing a central part of the Christian message. We must not
throw it away, but we must regain its original meaning."

It is quite true that the modern use of "vocation" and even
more of "vocational" seldom has the remotest reference to
religion. It means more or less simply "technical". So in
educational theory a "liberal" education is contrasted with a
"vocational" one. "Vocational" training is specialized preparation for a trade or profession, and the less relation it has
to "academic" culture the more specifically "vocational" it is
supposed to be.[2]

On the other hand, in this country at least, it has long been

---

[1] *The Divine Imperative*, pp. 205-6.
[2] "We attach no odium to vocational instruction." (*General Education in a Free Society*, Harvard Report, p. 52.)

customary to distinguish between a profession and a trade, and to distinguish both from a vocation. The distinction between the first two has to do partly with the cultural status of the professions sometimes described as "liberal", and partly with the different organization and standards of each. Tawney says a profession is organized for the performance of functions or duties, while a trade is organized for the protection of rights. He adds that "the difference between industry as it exists to-day and a profession is simple and unmistakable".[1] It has to do mostly with the relation of work done to its reward. In the professions, and especially in the public services, there are ethical standards of service and professional honour which do not admit that success is to be measured by money reward. Tawney sets before us as one of the main lines of social progress to elevate the trades up to the standards of honour and public service of the professions, so deposing the money interest from the dominant position, even if we cannot eliminate it altogether. He advocates a reorganization of society on a functional basis, where the lawless and predatory elements of industry are made responsible to public control, and individual rights are made subject to social purposes.

Tawney wrote before 1921 and the course of subsequent events has made it much more difficult to draw the lines that to him were "simple and unmistakable". This is partly due to the development of public ownership and control of the means of production, which has blurred the edges of trades and professions, and introduced new problems cutting across old barriers; partly also it is due to the refusal any longer to admit that even in the sphere of industry and trade men are, or should be, actuated solely by the profit motive, "nature red in tooth and claw", and to the widespread acknowledgment by both sides in industry that in earning a daily or a weekly wage, a man should consider himself and be treated as a public servant, contributing to a common cause, and

[1] *The Acquisitive Society*, p. 108.

18

not merely playing for his own hand in callous disregard of the needs and wishes of his fellows. But it is an easy thing to determine the market value of the product of labour compared with the attempt to assess the social value of the labour producing it. We are in the midst of a social and economic revolution which aims at deposing money from its recent supremacy in the world of affairs, in favour of welfare and the common good. No one knows how the professions will emerge from this, with their standards of honour and service enhanced or impaired, nor does anyone know how far "professional" standards can prevail in industry and raise the moral level of men's work and commercial dealing by interpreting them in terms of social duty.

But we may be quite sure that whatever arrangements are come to, for instance in the new medical service, it will not in any sense amount to "payment by results"; and we recognize at once that though it may be a desirable practice professionally to pay a doctor according to the number of visits, consultations, or operations, to pay a minister in proportion to the number of visits, services or conversions shown at the end of the year, would be even more incongruous than to pay a doctor only in proportion to his cures. But there are such things as minimum stipends, graded "supply" fees and various standards which are entirely proper and in fact necessary if a minister is to maintain his professional efficiency and abuses are to be prevented or minimized. Payment by results in a trade is or should be normal—"the adequate incentive"—in a profession it is inadvisable, and in a vocation, entirely incongruous.

Among men made in the image of God, no job should be a "mere" job, though in a world such as ours no vocation, even the ministry, can be a "pure" vocation. It is interesting how even in a trade it is often necessary to adopt a mixed system of "piece-work" and time rates. Even in a coal-mine it is not possible to pay everyone entirely according to output.

We shall have to consider the difference between "market values" and "vocation values", the inadvisability of allowing any sphere of human life and activity to be entirely ruled by the former, and the impossibility of ridding any "vocation", even the ministry, of all considerations of market values. We shall also see how, on a true spiritual construction, it is impossible to dissociate the three dictionary meanings of vocation, as if they could really be separated from one another. If the first dictionary meaning (1) be theologically construed as "election", such "election" on any true Christian interpretation must issue either in a sense of "mission" (2), in which a man leaves the market-place to devote himself to a "vocation", or (3) in a sense that his daily work is a "calling", in which he may serve and glorify God in his secular job. This third sense again is merely the more general outcome of a "call" of which the sense of "mission" is a particular instance. In other words, our task to-day is to lead men to make their choices and do their daily work, be they parsons or scavengers, with a sense of vocation and so to "work out their own salvation". But this is certainly not easy and it may not be possible for everyone regarded simply as an individual.

To-day Churches of all denominations, Roman, and Protestant, and Orthodox, are realizing how much the spiritual "sacred" world has become insulated and sterilized, while the "secular" world has degenerated into mere paganism, and are earnestly trying to recover the redeeming relevance of the Gospel to the facts of everyday life, and of our social patterns, as well as of our souls. We see also the very grave dangers of degeneration confronting all professions and trades in which the sense of a "calling" has grown weak. "One of the tragedies of our time has been the change of teaching from a calling to something like an industry."[1] "Soldiering is in danger of becoming a business rather than a vocation."[2] If it were merely the word vocation that was

---

[1] Harvard Report, p. 26
[2] Bernard Fergusson, *The Spectator*, July 28, 1950.

misused, comparatively little harm would be done, but it is when the sense of a call and of a calling passes out of human life that industrialism sets foot on the slope that leads downward to totalitarianism. The faith has got more to do with the job than we realized. And the faith "working out" in the job has got more to do with the set-up of the community than we realized. It is only when treated as a "cosmos of callings"[1] that the world can ever know real peace, in which liberty and order shall lie down together in a responsible society, whose citizens are free because in their souls and in their work the hand of God is plain.

Is it not the essence of the Gospel, and the message more than any other needed in our time, that we are living in a world where both persons and things have been made and are being made by a personal God with whom we can enter into personal relationships in faith and prayer? The whole Gospel, its Manger-Cradle, its Cross, its Empty Tomb, its Pentecost, is directed to make and restore personal relationships, in spite of human sin which creates barriers between man and God. And God puts meaning and purpose into our lives by His call and in our calling. If we are to be able to redeem men in our age of techniques and depersonalizing machinery, we must be able to make real to them the great truths of Creation, Providence and Grace, as these are personalized in the doctrine of vocation. Only so can we transmit the Gospel of redemption through the media of our age to rescue souls and build up the city of God.

[1] Troeltsch, *The Social Teaching of the Christian Churches*, I, p. 293.

Chapter Two

THE BIBLICAL DOCTRINE OF VOCATION

(A) The Vocation of Israel in the Old Testament

IT is a delusion common to almost every age of history to imagine that its problems and difficulties are unprecedented and quite peculiar to itself. But if anyone turns with an honest mind to the Old Testament he will find two things: first, that the whole furniture of life has changed beyond all recognition; and second, that in spite of that, the problems of the soul remain quite remarkably the same. It is a common remark among those who are preaching to the times with their finger on the pulse of life, that more and more they tend to preach from the Old Testament. That is a dangerous thing, for it may mean that they are sinking to a sub-Christian or pre-Christian attitude towards life. But it is also a significant thing, for it means that they find there revealed the great problems of the soul and its redemption, the destiny of nations, and the reality of Providence. It is not for nothing that the Old Testament is included in the canon of Scripture, and that the Gospel comes between the prophets and the Apostle Paul. We have perhaps been too narrowly concerned with the Jesus of history, to the conclusion or neglect of His own background in the history, the law, and the prophets of the Old Testament, and of the classical architecture of our faith, as in the Epistles. In consequence our religion has become weak and sentimental, and many of us are still living on the wrong side of Pentecost, content with a liberal humanism that lacks a message of redemption for our souls or for our times.

Paganism, though armed with all the material resources, the knowledge and skill of the twentieth century, does not differ spiritually from paganism as confronted by Abraham, by Moses, and by the prophets. Our idols are more complicated, our virtues and vices a little more sophisticated, and hypocrisy (the crowning vice of civilization) less easily detected. In the Old Testament, instead of elaborate arguments about the reality and personality of God, we have for the most part dramatic descriptions of the way people behaved for or against God, taking for granted most of the things we argue about to-day.

With Abraham, quite obviously, a new chapter began in the relations between God and man. That a man should at the "call" of God leave his home and kindred, his settled prospects, and tearing up all his roots, become a wanderer who never afterwards knew what a home was like, was till then an unheard-of thing. A new meaning was given to "faith", when it made a man behave like that. Indeed it was one of the turning-points in the history of the world. This man setting up his tent and his altar wherever he went is one of the greatest makers of history, and of religious experience, which is the heart of history. If we read Genesis, chapters 12–25, we realize how the whole human race really struck its tents and began to march with Abraham, choosing the strenuous life before the easy life, the tent before the brick house. And yet there were nomads before Abraham. He did not become a mere wanderer, but a pilgrim; it was no streak of gipsy blood in him that drove him out, but what he believed to be a direct command of God, a "call". *Abraham was the first man with a definite, explicit sense of vocation.* "Faith" ever afterwards was a response to a "call" from God, a personal relationship involving responsibility on both sides, the germ of the "covenant" idea that was the secret of Israel's greatness as a people, and is so still.

23

For, properly understood, the Old Testament is the Book of the Vocation of Israel, the "Chosen People" of God. The word "vocation" does not occur in the Authorized Version, except once in the New Testament (Eph. 4: 1), nor does the noun "call" occur in the A.V., but the verb "to call" with its derivatives in various meanings is frequently used with a wide range of meaning, from merely addressing by name to the full sense of a Christian "vocation", as it developed through the Old into the New Testament. The idea is fundamental to the whole message of Scripture. Over against the background of idolatry and witchcraft, and all the sinister and ugly things involved in the crude religions round about, this new, strong, and beautiful kind of personal relationship between God and man shines out like a good deed in a naughty world. Indeed it was so lofty and severe that the Israelites often felt unable to live up to it, and slipped back into the grey mass of heathen idolatry and wickedness around them.

It is easy for superior people to explain away this covenant sense of a personal relationship between God and His chosen people, of a Call and its response in faith. If an unsophisticated people imagined it all, as a projection of material ambition, a piece of wishful thinking, then look at the subsequent history of this supposed illusion. In the Prophets it reached the loftiest heights of religious experience and insight anywhere in the history of the world, except in the New Testament. In the Psalms it provided the world with its finest book of devotion. Greatest achievement of all, it was taken up and transformed into the fuller revelation of the New Testament. When somebody told Abraham Lincoln that General Grant, the only one of his generals who could win battles, was a hard drinker, Lincoln asked for the name of the stuff that Grant drank, so that he could send some to his other generals! If Israel's sense of vocation be illusion, would to God the whole world were filled with such illusions, which have so enriched mankind! But the realist

24

insists on pragmatic evidence. Then let him examine the history of Israel, its incomparable power of spiritual endurance, its magnificent contribution to the spiritual wealth of the human race. The Greeks and Romans have had their day, and ceased to be. Their gifts to us and to all men remain, to constitute an enriched civilization, but they themselves as great nations have perished in the giving of them. But the Jews have made their contribution, and still endure, because the soul of their people was something stronger than law, philosophy, or culture, namely religion. They have broken all the rules for the natural behaviour of nations in their rise and wane. They lost their land, their independence, their political entity, everything but their integrity based on their religion. There is no parallel to their strange pertinacity, save that other mystery of miraculous quality, the Church of Christ. And the end of these things is not yet.

Their sense of vocation has made the Jews a people, has kept them still a people. When they lose their sense of vocation they will cease to be a people. Meanwhile the time has not yet come when we can assess our debt to them. We cannot compare incommensurables, such as the relative importance of Greeks, Romans, and Jews, especially as the Jewish contribution has been largely indirect through Christianity. It is perhaps wisest to consider the three as the permanent dimensions of every European civilization worthy of the name. To eliminate one of these, as Hitler and others tried to do in their persecution of the Jews, is to slip back from a civilization of three dimensions into one of two, without full reality or power to maintain itself in the modern world.

This is not the place to describe the religion of the Old Testament, or to trace its development. This covenant sense of a national vocation had its aspect of privilege and its aspect of responsibility. The children of Israel, like all human beings, attempted time and again to evade the responsibilities and seize the privileges, to assure themselves of the favour of

God, which made them safe and prosperous, while forgetting their obligations towards one another and their missionary duty towards other peoples. Alone among the people of antiquity, they had a God who was to be relied on. But the reverse of this, not always palatable, was that because of this God was always to be reckoned with, and could not be deceived. He demanded of His peculiar people conduct befitting those in this unique relation to a holy God. As W. M. Macgregor puts it in an unforgettable phrase: "The elementary law of Christian living, for laymen just as much as for the cleric, is that, having come through Jesus to know the Father, we are put here on our honour to live such lives as match our discovery."[1]

This sense of personal relationship to God and absolute responsibility to Him Christianity inherited from the Jews.

So much of what they taught us has passed into the common furniture of our minds and our worship that we quite fail to realize how far their religious experience advanced beyond the capricious deities and magic rites around them. The paganism of our day is the paganism of mechanism: the paganism of the Old Testament is a paganism of magic. But idolatry is pretty much the same, whether we worship Baal or a deified nation state. "Are we, or are we not, going to worship the work of our own hands?" (A. D. Lindsay). And the moral results of idolatry are always the same, whatever the work of men's hands that they set up to worship. The paganism of mechanism confronts us to-day with its ruthless impersonality, the paganism of magic was equally and similarly impersonal. Both alike destroy the soul.

Over against all that the God of the Israelites had two aspects. Instead of the fickleness of the gods who could be manipulated by magic was the holiness of Jehovah, so remote in His majesty from human imperfection that even His name must not be mentioned. We do not know to this day how to pronounce the word that we wrongly write as

[1] *For Christ and the Kingdom*, p. 65.

Jehovah. No Israelite would dare to take that sacred name upon his lips.[1] But this holiness was a positive and a moral thing. The elaborate scheme of propitiation so prominent in the Old Testament was not an attempt to hoodwink or buy off a malevolent God, such as the animists fear, but a costly attempt to bridge the deep gulf between man's sinfulness and God's holiness. His attitude to His Chosen People was one of loving kindness; His thoughts were thoughts of peace towards them, and not of evil. And as a complement to this transcendent view of Jehovah, inaccessible and remote in His holiness, was the other view of the "God of Abraham, the God of Isaac, and the God of Jacob". In Exodus, chapter 3, we see both "transcendent" and "immanent" views set down together as elements in one revelation. Whatever actually happened at the Burning Bush, the effects of it are still powerfully affecting our lives. This name for God so beautifully woven from their forefather's names, as a token that God dwelt with each of them as personally and intimately as a man dwells and deals with his friend, is another turning-point of history, indeed it is the next important milestone after Abraham's "Call".

But there is even more than that in it. It shows us God, dealing with each generation of man, with one continuing, increasing, prevailing purpose. That, to us Christians at least, is the very meaning of history, though it was not so recognized till St. Augustine, who has been well described as "the first man with a sense of time"!

Both these new names for God contain the origin of what we call the modern view of history, according to which human affairs are neither static, mere repetitions of an outworn tale, where nothing new ever arises, nor are they aimless, capricious, and irrational accidental events. Behind all happenings lies a personal purpose, based on the constancy of an Almighty Will, that works through the generations

[1] But on this see Snaith, *Distinctive Ideas of the Old Testament*, especially pp. 24-32; 79-80.

27

without reducing the personalities of history to mere pup-
pets—in other words, the view of Providence (another word
that occurs only once in the Authorized Version, and there
referring to human foresight, yet a dominant theme of
Scripture). With all deference to Herodotus, Thucydides,
and others, it is the Jews who have taught us our philosophy
of history, though they were no philosophers themselves.
Their distinctive contribution to the history of religion came
through the prophets, who were men "called" to a special
mission by God.[1]

The nation had its "call" from God: but within the nation
God had personal dealings with those called to special
duties. The Burning Bush, Mount Sinai and many other
incidents illustrate this personal relationship between
Jehovah and His Chosen People and its leaders. God
"called" the nation through its representatives, who thus
had a "call" in the second sense.

The typical illustration or *locus classicus* of this is the Call
of Isaiah (Isa. 6). Close study of the chapter shows how the
first two senses of vocation are emphasized, the Call to surrender and penitence issuing in a "mission".[2]

God spoke to the nation and through them to other
nations, by inspiring the prophets (e.g. Amos, chapter 7,
Isaiah 6, 1 Samuel 3); but kings (Saul: 1 Samuel 9 and 10;
David: 1 Samuel 16); and priests (Exodus 28 and 29) were
also "called", designated by name for their special duties. So
"catholic" was the view of the prophets as to the world-
wide purpose of God that they even claimed as among the
"called of God", or at least as agents of Providence, un-
believers who were outside the Covenant, such as Naaman
(2 Kings 5: 1), and Cyrus (Isaiah 44: 28, and 45: 1).

Two of the three senses of vocation which we discovered

---

[1] See John Baillie, *The Belief in Progress*, especially pp. 6 ff., pp. 54 ff., and
pp. 186-235. "It is only among the Hebrews that we find any conception of
history as a significant process" (p. 65). See also Collingwood, *The Idea of
History*, p. 48 f., quoted by John Baillie, *ibid.*, p. 187 n.

[2] "All revelation is summons and sending". M. Buber, *I and Thou*, p. 115.

in modern usage of the word are already plainly developed
in the Old Testament: (1) the "Call" of God to His "Chosen"
People, the people in covenant with Him, sharing in that
fellowship; and (2) the "call" to the prophets and others
designated for special office or duty, a special "commission"
in accordance with special capacities, something not intended for everybody; (3) we have not yet got more than
hints of the sense of a "calling" as it was later laid down by
Jesus and by Paul and much later still developed by the
Reformers. The particular treatment of "the secular calling"
must wait till Part Two of this book.

(B) *The Vocation of Jesus in the New Testament*

There are very few, if any, ideas in the New Testament
that do not have their roots in the Old. So this thought of
vocation is caught up and transfigured in the case of Jesus,
who claims to stand in the direct descent of the long line of
the prophets. This is the meaning of the great crisis of His
public ministry, the Transfiguration, coming as it does in all
the Synoptic Gospels immediately after Peter's discovery
of the Christ in the carpenter (Matthew 16: 13–23; Mark 8:
27–33; Luke 9: 18–22). When Peter, James and John, the
three Jesus had chosen out of the twelve who were "called"
to be His most intimate disciples, were confronted by Moses
and Elijah in converse with Jesus, we see two things: (1)
the continuity between those great figures of Israel's past
and the "mission" of Jesus; and (2) the beginning of the
"mission" of these disciples, who in the name of Christ
were to carry forward the work He had inherited from His
people's past history, and their vocation from God.

(1) Many scholars have attempted a close study of the
vocation of Jesus. On every page of the Gospels we find
evidence that He considered Himself to be "sent" to do a
particular work. The different titles given Him—"the
Christ", "the Son of David", "the Son of Man", "the Son
of God"—have each their special significance as to what He

claimed and what was attributed to Him. "My Father worketh hitherto, and I work" (John 5: 17); "For thereto am I sent" (Luke 4: 43). He is constantly at pains to assert and reiterate that He is come to fulfil and complete the work of the prophets, to do what He has been commissioned to do, to establish the Kingdom of God upon the earth. "Realized eschatology"—the theory that the Kingdom has already been established, that it is no mere ideal floating in the air, or in the future—is a fascinating and difficult subject, but there can be no doubt that from the time of Peter's confession and the Transfiguration Jesus's teaching takes a new turn. The previous demand for insight gives place to a demand for loyalty.[1] Peter's confession is "the watershed of the Gospel history". Once recognized by the disciples as the Christ, the Anointed of God, He goes on to lead them towards the Cross and the Resurrection, in which He fulfilled His vocation; He was sent by God to become the Saviour of the World.[2]

In this idea of vocation we find the clue not merely to the Transfiguration, but also to such experiences as the baptism and temptation of Jesus, Gethsemane and the Cross itself. "The real significance of the temptations lies in their bearing upon the vocation of Jesus."[3] The baptism and the temptation taken together reveal Jesus's complete identification of Himself and His mission, both with the purpose of God as already revealed through the prophets, and with the condition of man disabled by his sinfulness. He was "baptized into a sense of the condition of all men". The whole Gospel story becomes luminous when we see this. Almost every recorded incident and saying has some immediate reference to it. Jesus was not a man of remarkable spiritual powers with big and ambitious ideas, but a man under orders. We see in Him in a unique way the difference between self-

---

[1] See T. W. Manson, *The Teaching of Jesus*, p. 201.
[2] See G. S. Duncan, *Jesus, Son of Man*, especially Part II, Chap. X
[3] T. W. Manson, *ibid.*, p. 196.

assertion and a true sense of vocation. In anyone else the claims He made, on any interpretation of them, would have been ridiculous even to blasphemy. "His unique vocation", says Ritschl, "is to establish the Kingdom of God." For this end He consecrated Himself at the baptism and in Gethsemane. In spite of its obvious chronological difficulties, the Gospel story forms a remarkable spiritual unity when seen in the light of this great principle of vocation, though as a handbook of ethics or system of theological ideas it leaves so much to be desired. The strong and undoubted authority of Jesus, in which He differed so far from the Scribes and Pharisees, claiming for Himself and demanding from others far more than these supposed religious authorities dared to do, is traced by Him to the source of His mission. His powers were given Him by His Father to enable Him to do the work He had been sent to do. He refused to quote chapter and verse for everything He did, or said, or expected, as the Pharisees did. Like Paul, the greatest of His followers, He claimed to derive His power, not from Himself, nor from or through man, but directly from the God whom he called Father, and taught His disciples to call Father, whose purpose of salvation had sent Him into the world, and led Him to the Cross and beyond. It cannot be said that there was never any perplexity or discouragement in His life, that He always marched breast forward and never hesitated. If He had, there would have been something lacking in His partaking of our flesh and blood. Gethsemane and the cry of forsakenness on the Cross show that He tasted the dregs of suffering and shared in the sense of being cut off from God that sin brings to us and that sin-bearing brought with inconceivable dreadfulness to Him. But He went through with it, for there was no other way to fulfil the purpose for which He had been sent.

(2) Now the testing time for any new idea is when its discoverer dies, and his followers attempt to continue his work. Earth's human shores are littered with the wrecks of

splendid armadas that carried all before them till their leader died, and then, deprived of his genius, the cause went all astray. An important part of the genius of a real leader of men is the power of choosing subordinates who will translate his ideas and orders into actual realities, and of training others to carry on the movement when its founder is gone.

Here Jesus does not seem to the worldly eye to have been very successful. He gathered round Him a considerable number of undistinguished followers, and out of them He chose twelve plain and rather ignorant and ungifted men. Within that small number again there were three who seem to have been specially privileged, Peter, James and John. None of these seemed to possess the aptitude for carrying on the work even on the modest scale on which it was begun by Jesus Himself, nor would anyone have suspected that little band of becoming a world-transforming power. Jesus did not even take the obvious precaution of committing His more important instructions to writing in some permanent form. He wrote nothing at all, so far as is recorded, except once some characters in sand.

This is not the place to describe the transformation of the disciples, when the Holy Spirit came at Pentecost, or their clumsy early attempts at formulating the Gospel whose nature and implications were slowly dawning on them. Then came Paul, next to Jesus the best instance in Scripture of a man with a sense of vocation. From the manner of his conversation and God's wonderful way in dealing with him, Paul never had any doubt as to his "call". After Pentecost, to the astonishment of everyone, the remarkable spiritual power men had seen in the person of Jesus now possessed His disciples, through His Spirit. So John, writing after this fact had become obvious, reports Jesus as saying: "As Thou hast sent me into the world, even so have I also sent them into the world" (John 17: 18).[1]

[1] On the close "analogy between His experience of God and ours" see D. M. Baillie, *God Was in Christ*, especially pp. 127-132. It is one of the many

The confidence with which those early disciples faced their enemies in Church and State, a confidence entirely different from the assertiveness of able men with ambitious ideas, was the proof that the plain man, inspired by the Holy Spirit, acquired this sense of vocation that made him able to confront and overcome all resistance without losing either his head or his soul.

A glance at the beginning of most of the epistles of St. Paul (e.g. Romans 1: 6, 7; 1 Cor. 1: 1, 2; Galatians 1: 1-6; Ephesians 1: 1, 4, 5, 6; 1 Thess. 2: 12; 1 Timothy 1: 1 and 7; 2 Timothy 1: 1, 9; Titus 1: 1) shows that in spite of differences of phraseology Paul generally began his letters with an assertion of his authority as "one called to be an apostle". That was his commission. It had come to him directly from his Master at his conversion on the way to Damascus, he did not owe it to the mediation of any man. He never questioned the authority of the One who appeared to him then, or the authenticity of the command to be the apostle of the Gentiles. He frequently followed up this claim by addressing the church to which he is writing as "called to be saints". In the current phraseology of to-day a "saint" is a person of great "saintliness" of character—"saints" are commonly contrasted with "sinners". But that is not the Scripture meaning of the word. In the New Testament it means one who accepts the offer of salvation, who stands in fellowship with God and with his fellow Christians in the society of the redeemed. It is not surprising that instead of this formula "called to be saints", St. Paul should sometimes use "the elect", or some similar word indicating predestination. *In St. Paul predestination, as the background of Christian life, takes the place of the covenant in the Old Testament.* Difficult though

excellences of this admirable book that it draws attention to the close relation of the problem of the Person of Christ to the problem of Christian faith, conscience and character. Let us hope the author will continue to pursue the analogy, even if it involves a further "paradox" in the double nature of the Church as a divine ordinance and a human institution, both the Body of Christ and the body of our humiliation.

C   33

the conception of predestination is, its positive sense is vocation, this call of God to Salvation, the Gospel of grace as it was proclaimed by Jesus and responded to in the faith of those who became His disciples (Romans 8: 28–39).

We see then how very closely the two chief meanings of vocation in the Old Testament persist in the New, with the transformation of all spiritual values effected by Jesus. (1) Instead of the Chosen People in covenant relation with Jehovah, we have the "ecclesia", the assembly of the redeemed; "the elect", those who have accepted salvation, and are now working it out in their own lives day by day. The Church inherits the promises made to Israel and accepts her missionary responsibility to evangelize the world.

(2) The apostle is not merely called in that general sense, but he has his special "call" or commission to specified duties. Turn to Ephesians 4, and you will find (in the only mention of the *word* vocation in our Authorized Version) that this principle provides for and explains the diversity of function within the Church, the Body of Christ. The thought (though not the word) dominates the other treatments of the same theme in Romans 12 and 1 Corinthians 12, in speaking of the "diversities of gifts" and "differences of administration". All do not have the same gifts, nor do they have the same vocation. The Body of Christ is "edified" when each discovers his vocation and faithfully performs it. We shall see later on how vastly important this is as a principle of social integration.

(3) But we owe to St. Paul the first formulation in history of a principle of which we have only hints even in the Old Testament, when, in 1 Corinthians 7, he tells us that a man's daily work may be, and in fact ought to be, ordained for him by God, and that our business is to discover our "calling". You will observe in this chapter (vv. 17–31) how the apostle treats the difference between the circumcised Jew and the

34

uncircumcised Gentile, between slavery and freedom, be-between marriage and virginity, as one of vocation. Each of those conditions is at once a state in which we must "abide", and a sphere in which we must serve and glorify God. There are negative and positive senses of the words "To abide in your calling", for God has put you there, means that if you are a servant, even a slave, you must do your work there faithfully, remembering that you are one of the freemen of God. If you are a freeman, consider yourself the bond-servant of God. "Ye are bought with a price; be not the servants of men. Brethren, let every man, wherein he is called, there abide with God."

This apparently negative meaning is counterbalanced by a positive one, namely the new motive that this puts into one's daily work. "Quite deliberately he (Paul) places these secular conditions and circumstances—the profession or status a man happens to be in at the time of his conversion—on the same spiritual level as that conversion itself. Each is a "call" or "calling" direct from God. To express this the apostle is forced to use the Greek word *klēsis* in an entirely new sense; for no strict parallel to the use of "calling" for secular "avocation" . . . can be found in contemporary literature. . . . It is to Paul that we owe the great Christian truth that the most ordinary and secular employment can and should be regarded as a mission directly laid upon us by the Omnipotent God Himself."[1]

Those who think that the Bishop of Oxford is reading too much into this passage, should put it alongside the teaching of Jesus, especially the emphasis on stewardship in the parables. Paul is not allowing free rein to an over-fertile imagination. He is merely following in the footsteps of his Master. This great claim that our "secular" employments are, should, and can be, "calls" and "callings" from God, is the great principle governing the relation of the sacred to the secular. This is the third of the three chief meanings of this

[1] K. E. Kirk, *The Vision of God*, pp. 81, 82.

great principle as it is treated in Scripture. And it is this principle alone which can enable us to deal redeemingly with the tragic errors of our time.

Chapter Three

ARE THERE TWO STANDARDS OF MORALITY?

ONE of the perplexing things about the New Testament is the way in which it seems to look forward to an imminent *parousia* or return of our Lord in judgment, when the world will come to an end. Hence even in St. Paul for all his far-sightedness there is no long-term policy. "The time is short;" "The fashion of this world passeth away" (e.g. 1 Cor. 7: 29, 31, etc.). It is quite possible that in recent years this doctrine of the *parousia* has been over-emphasized, as if it explained away some of the urgency of the Gospel for our own day. It is equally possible to explain Jesus' teaching on the subject as fulfilled (*a*) by the Resurrection, and (*b*) by the coming of the Holy Spirit at Pentecost. But we cannot explain away this belief of the early Church, for it was undoubtedly responsible for the way in which Christian teaching developed and new patterns of social behaviour and of the structure of the Church began to take shape. In the New Testament all arrangements in founding the Church are "interim", almost emergency provisions. There is little or no sense of the need or possibility of reforming a world-order which is presumably soon to pass away. All the emphasis is rightly put on evangelism. And similarly, though we have a great deal of discussion especially in the Epistles of matters of conduct, there is a good deal to be said for those who maintain that such rules as were laid down were only an "interim-ethic" till the forthcoming "day of the

Lord".[1] It is an urgent "morality of crisis", mobilized if you like, based on the example and sayings of Jesus. It is fascinating to see in the Epistles the way in which the little groups of Christian believers are trying to translate these principles into policies, to insert their new kind of faith and its new patterns of conduct and fellowship into the intricacies of heathen social and political life in the Graeco-Roman world. In the Book of the Revelation this morality of crisis is apparently in its most acute form on the brink of world-catastrophe. Christian disciples must avoid all entanglements with the world.

Before we pass from the New Testament itself we find evidence of the difficulty the first Christian disciples found in reconciling what is called the "love-perfectionism of the Gospels", with the necessities and possibilities of life in the social, political and economic circumstances of their time. In 1 Corinthians 7, we find Paul very much troubled about difficult questions of marriage, divorce and sex relationships generally. His diffident conclusions (see vv. 6 and 40), taken along with v. 17 f., suggest that already a distinction was being drawn in this regard between those who aimed at "perfection", and those who were content with a second-best, the right course in each case being determined by special "gifts" and a special "vocation".

The same is true about the early Church's first attempts to apply the teaching of Jesus, "sell that thou hast", to the possession of property. In the story of Ananias and Sapphira in Acts 5, there is no suggestion that everyone was obliged to sell all their property and apply the proceeds in whole or in part to Church purposes. But undoubtedly this "communist" experiment, if such it may be called, was a kind of "counsel of perfection", recommended to those with heroic spiritual ambitions. We know that the Church at Jerusalem fell into

[1] There is also a great deal to be said for Brunner's contention that "all genuine Protestant Ethics is 'interim ethics'" (*The Divine Imperative*, p. 123). We are still living "between the times", the Kingdom has been established, the Kingdom has not yet reached final victory.

grave poverty, it became dependent on the charity of the other Churches. But the evidence does not enable us to say with any confidence that it was impoverished by its "communistic experiment". More probably its prominent members were mostly forced to flee, and what we have recorded was not an experiment in communism but an attempt at literal interpretation of certain precepts of the Gospel by certain individuals, leading again to the inference that some were striving after perfection, while the rest were content to accept a less heroic course of conformity to more normal ways of living.

We must not under-estimate the extremely difficult tasks that confronted the early Christians, and in all their literature of this period we may trace this uneasiness, especially in three directions: (1) the sex ethic; (2) the property ethic, and (3) the whole State ethic, which came to a head in the question whether a Christian could enter the army and take part in war. It cannot be maintained that the Christian Church as such ever took up a pacifist attitude either before or after Constantine, though certain prominent leaders made pronouncements that would to-day be called "pacifist". It is difficult to discover exactly how much of the widespread uneasiness on the subject was due to the element of violence inherent in the soldier's life, and how much to the incompatibility of his *sacramentum*, the soldier's oath of absolute obedience, with the Christian's *sacramentum* as a disciple of Jesus. The soldiers were expected to take a prominent part in the Emperor worship. The Roman claims were totalitarian. We know that similar difficulties led at times to searchings of heart as to whether a Christian could act as a teacher of the pagan classics or could be a sailor or a magistrate. We shall return to this problem of pacifism in Chapter Five.

From very early times we can trace the tendency to set up two different standards of morality, based more or less explicitly on a certain interpretation of Matthew 19, 16–30. There the rich young ruler is apparently told that to "enter into life" it is sufficient to "keep the commandments", but if he wants to be "perfect" he must "sell that thou hast". On this interpretation, apparently supported by certain other sayings of Jesus and St. Paul, those who aim at perfection must adopt the ascetic life of poverty, celibacy, and absolute non-resisting obedience, while those who merely desire to "enter the kingdom" may go on living in families, owning property, and in other ways conforming to the structure and conventions of life in the world, so long as they keep the commandments.

There is no trace anywhere in St. Paul that for the masses of men moral mediocrity or an ethical minimum is all that is required of disciples, while spiritual distinction is reserved for an *élite*. In 1 Corinthians 7, we see a curious diffidence in the Apostle's unwillingness to claim divine authority for judgments and opinions on matters which are beyond his experience, coupled with an injunction to avoid entanglement in a world soon to pass away, and a strong leaning towards asceticism. It is all the more interesting that we should have in the midst of this chapter the important passage already quoted, p. 38 (vv. 17–24). "But, as the Lord has distributed to every man, as the Lord has called every man, so let him walk. . . . Brethren, let every man, wherein he is called, therein abide with God." Bishop Kirk may be right in claiming that here for the first time in literature we have an explicit doctrine of vocation in daily life. There is no parallel in classical Greek to the thought that a man's occupation and place in society are intended to be the means by which he is enabled to glorify God. The nearest we get to such a thought is in Epictetus.[1] But, as Joh. Weiss remarks, after giving the references, what Epictetus gives is "a formula for inner spiritual freedom, not to be disturbed by external circumstances, a very different thing from the positive and truly 'vocational' teaching of the Apostle".[2] A much closer

[1] *Discourses*, I xxix, 33–49; II vi, 18; IV vi, 21; V, 22; III xxii, 37
[2] Meyer, *Kom. zum N.T.*, *I Kor. Brief.*, Joh. Weiss, p. 127.

parallel is to be found in the early Christian letter *Ad Diogne-tum* (dated *c.* 130–150), where we see how the very thing the Apostle indicated was working out in practice. Here we have no theory, but a record of the difference men observed in the little Christian communities of transformed, dedicated men and women:

> For Christians are not distinguished from the rest of man-kind either in locality or in speech or in customs. For they dwell not somewhere in cities of their own, neither do they use some different language, nor practice an extraordinary kind of life. Nor again do they possess any invention discovered by any intelligence or study of ingenious men, nor are they masters of any human dogma as some are. But while they dwell in cities of Greeks and barbarians as the lot of each is cast, and follow native customs in dress and food and the other arrangements of life, yet the constitution of their own citizen-ship, which they set forth, is marvellous, and confessedly con-tradicts expectation. They dwell in their own countries, but only as sojourners; they bear their share in all things as citizens, and they endure all hardships as strangers, every foreign coun-try is a fatherland to them, and every fatherland is foreign. They marry like all other men, and they beget children; but they do not cast away their offspring. They have their meals in com-mon, but not their wives. They find themselves in the flesh, and yet they live not after the flesh. Their existence is on earth, but their citizenship is in Heaven.[1]

You will notice from the lists of activities of human life in which the Christians joined, and which they transformed, that they did not draw apart into a segregated life, but shared in the common lot, yet with a difference. They had what we nowadays would call a sense of vocation, of being called by God to undertake responsibilities, to occupy posts of honour and no honour, without allowing their choices and their be-haviour to be determined by earthly standards.

The Epistle goes on to make this clear: "Broadly speaking, what the soul is in the body, that Christians are in the world. The soul is dispersed through all the members of the body,

---

[1] Lightfoot, *The Apostolic Fathers*, pp. 505–6.

and Christians throughout the cities of the world. The soul dwells in the body, but is not of the body; and Christians dwell in the world, but 'are not of the world'. The soul, itself invisible, is guarded in the body which is visible; so Christians are known as being in the world, but their religion remains unseen. . . . Christians sojourn among corruptible things, awaiting the incorruptibility which is in heaven."[1] We have here a doctrine of the relation of the Church to the world which is the inevitable counterpart of St. Paul's great doctrine of the Church as the Body of Christ. For centuries this metaphor was the favourite description of the relations of the Church to the State. There are elements of important truth in such a correlation, though if the metaphor is pressed into a principle and the Church is identified with the ecclesiastical institution, the metaphor leads us, as it led so many then, into the autocratic pretensions of Romanism.

If this letter was written about 150 A.D., and represents the authentic way in which Christian faith was working itself out in the ways of common life, how comes it then that within less than 200 years, Eusebius could write that there were two kinds of Christian behaviour, each with a different standard, by which it was to be judged: (1) the life of those who would be perfect, to whom religion meant separation from all secular interests and employments; and (2) the life of those who remained in the world, who might marry, fight in the army and, most important for our purpose, were allowed to have minds for farming, for trade and the other more secular interests, as well as for religion? And "a kind of secondary grade of piety (alone) is attributed to them . . .". That the Christian Life is of Two Distinct Characters.[2]

The one [Moses] wrote on lifeless tables, the Other wrote the perfect commandments of the new covenant on living minds. And His disciples, accommodating their teaching to

[1] Meecham, *The Epistle to Diognetus p.* 81
[2] Eusebius, *Demonstratio Evangelica*, Book I, Chap. VIII. The chapter headings for Book I cannot with certainty be attributed to Eusebius himself, though they are very early (Ferrar's edition, p. xl).

the minds of the people, according to the Master's will, delivered on the one hand to those who were able to receive it,
the teaching given by the perfect master to those who rose
above human nature. While on the other the side of the teaching which they considered was suitable to men still in the
world of passion and needing treatment, they accommodated
to the weakness of the majority, and handed over to them to
keep sometimes in writing, and sometimes by unwritten
ordinances to be observed by them. Two ways of life were
thus given by the law of Christ to His Church. The one is
above nature, and beyond common human living; it admits
not marriage, child-bearing, property nor the possession of
wealth, but, wholly and permanently separate from the common customary life of mankind, it devotes itself to the service
of God alone in its wealth of heavenly love! And they who
enter on this course, appear to die to the life of mortals, to
bear with them nothing earthly but their body, and in mind
and spirit to have passed to heaven. Like some celestial beings
they gaze upon human life, performing the duty of a priesthood to Almighty God for the whole race, not with sacrifices
of bulls and blood, nor with libations and unguents, nor with
smoke and consuming fire and destruction of bodily things,
but with the right principles of true holiness, and of a soul
purified in disposition, and above all with virtuous deeds and
words; with such they propitiate the Divinity, and celebrate
their priestly rites for themselves and their race. Such then is
the perfect form of the Christian life. And the other, more
humble, more human, permits men to join in pure nuptials
and to produce children, to undertake government, to give
orders to soldiers fighting for right; it allows them to have
minds for farming, for trade, and the other more secular
interests as well as for religion; and it is for them that times
of retreat and instruction, and days for hearing sacred things
are set apart. And a kind of secondary grade of piety is attributed to them, giving just such help as such lives require,
so that all men, whether Greeks or barbarians, have their part
in the coming of salvation, and profit by the teaching of the
Gospel.

If this was written between 314 and 318 A.D., as is probable, we get an interesting contrast to the Epistle *Ad Diognetum*. We are living in a different spiritual atmosphere, and
it is not merely the change from a *persecuted* religion, as

Christianity was when the Epistle *Ad Diognetum* was written, to a *privileged* religion, as it was when Eusebius wrote. (He was the favourite of Constantine, who made Christianity the official religion of the Roman Empire in 313 A.D.)

The change is much more fundamental. From the very start the Christian Church had found difficulty in living the kind of life they believed their Christian faith required of them, in the circumstances first of Jewish and then of the Graeco-Roman civilization, in which the Church gained its first footing. We see this already in the Gospels (e.g. Matt. 10: 16, etc.), in the Acts of the Apostles, and in the letters of St. Paul and others. Once the first enthusiasm with its tense expectation of the coming again of Christ began to abate, the Church had to settle down alongside pagan neighbours, sometimes in the same house with pagan husbands or wives, and so forth,[1] and had to try to translate the Gospel into workable terms.

When a suitable compromise was secured, which saved them from open persecution at the cost of some conformity or other, there was frequently someone or some section who would not accept this settlement and wanted the whole Gospel, and what is known as "love-perfectionism" in all affairs and relationships in which they took part in this mixed society. Just about the time at which Eusebius was writing, Anthony, Pachomius, and others, were trying experiments in withdrawing from the relativities of life in the world to attempt the "absolute" ethic based on the Sermon on the Mount, either in isolation as hermits or in communities of monks.

Further, as Christianity began to spread, it made contact with Greek thought, with its tendency to disparage everything material, including the human body. Oriental asceticism, which it also met, seemed to point in the same direction, so that almost from the beginning certain individuals and

[1] See 1 Cor. 7 and elsewhere, and C. J. Cadoux, *The Early Church and the World, passim.*

groups tried to escape from the inevitable compromise of social, political and business life, into the simplicity of the desert life of the anchorite or the group, with a common life, spending all their time in striving after perfection. In practice such individuals and groups seemed to be obeying the words of Jesus and imitating as nearly as might be His actual attitudes, in theory Greek philosophy was (directly and through Egyptian and other sources—e.g. Philo) infecting Christian thinking and teaching about moral values and introducing the Greek aristocratic hauteur under the guise of an exegesis of Matthew 19. Those who aimed at perfection had to separate themselves from the world, to live celibate lives, hold no property, etc., while those who remained "in the world" were allowed to conform and required only to obey the Commandments (Matthew 19: 16–30). Perfection was not for them, but they still "had their part in the coming of salvation, and profit by the teaching of the Gospel". (Eusebius, *ibid.*) The sacred and secular on this view differed not merely in degree but in kind. Within the monastery or convent, the "religious" who had a "vocation" aimed at perfection, devoted themselves largely (though not exclusively) to contemplation, while outside in the family, in the market-place, in the field and on the seas, the others kept the wheels of the work of the world running, at the cost of condemning their souls to a second-best spiritual life.[1] The change between *Ad Diognetum* and Eusebius has been well described by Edwyn Bevan as one of "curdling", in a passage so illuminating that it deserves quotation:

> In quite early days every Christian had felt that Christianity made an immense demand upon him and he had had to be ready at any moment to forgo, for the sake of Christ and the Gospel, the things upon which the hearts of men were ordinarily set. But now that external conformity to Christianity had

[1] St. Thomas Aquinas quotes Aristotle as his authority (*Eth. Nic.* X: viii, 5, 6) that the life of activity requires more exterior goods than the contemplative life and therefore in the preoccupation such a life involves, evangelical simplicity is more difficult. Aquinas *Summa*, II: II, Q, CLXXXVIII, Art. vii.

become so much easier, we see the aspiration, the bent to renunciation, which had once run through the whole Christian body, concentrate itself in smaller groups separated from the rest of the body. It is like the phenomenon of curdling, when instead of the milk having a uniform consistency right through, some of its constituents coagulate and leave the rest watery. Perhaps it was the only way, in the circumstances of the time, by which a Christian life of distinct quality could be saved, but the curdling has entailed a difficulty for Catholicism ever since —the difficulty of the double standard in the Christian life. It has since then seemed possible to be a Christian and deliberately choose a manner of life lower than the highest. Since the charge of recognizing such a double standard has been one of those most persistently urged by Protestants against Catholics in the last four centuries, it may be in place here to try to make the points at issue clearer. That in the Christian body there are differences of function is agreed on both sides. Nor can Protestants consistently deny that some functions are more honourable than others, or that, if the voluntary endurance of great pains and privations is required for the performance of certain functions, those who perform them stand higher than ordinary Christians in the Church's roll of honour. Missionaries, for instance, who have done their work at the cost of great sufferings and renunciations are habitually held up in Protestant religious literature as Christian "heroes". The charge really brought against Catholics is not that they recognize such a difference between higher and lower kinds of Christian service but that they seem to make it optional for each individual whether he adopts the higher or the lower life. According to the Protestant theory, each individual has a particular work allotted to him by God, and to perform that faithfully is the highest thing which he can possibly do: it is wrong for anyone to aim at any standard lower than the highest possible for *him*. In a battle those detached for some operation which requires extraordinary endurance and courage perform a service in itself more glorious than that of those appointed to a post outside the danger-zone; yet the most meritorious work which those in the safe position can do is the work assigned them. The Catholic may reply that this view is precisely the one implied in his doctrine of "vocation": certain individuals only are "called" by God to the monastic life, and it would be wrong for anyone else to adopt it without such "vocation". Now if this idea of "vocation" were consistently carried through, the difference

46

between the Catholic and the Protestant view would perhaps disappear: then in Catholicism the individual would not be offered the option between a higher and a lower mode of life.[1]

We need not subscribe to Edwyn Bevan's optimism, but we cannot deny the importance of this distinction as it applies to Roman and Protestant belief and conduct. Another witness to the growth of this distinction is Clement of Alexandria:[2]

> ... man has been otherwise constituted by nature, so as to have fellowship with God. As, then, we do not compel the horse to plough, or the bull to hunt, but set each animal to that for which it is by nature fitted; so, placing our finger on what is man's peculiar and distinguishing characteristic above other creatures, we invite him—born, as he is, for the contemplation of heaven, and being, as he is, a truly heavenly plant—to the knowledge of God, counselling him to furnish himself with what is his sufficient provision for eternity, namely piety. Practise husbandry, we say, if you are a husbandman; but while you till your fields, know God. Sail the sea, you who are devoted to navigation, yet call the whilst on the heavenly Pilot. Has knowledge taken hold of you while engaged in military service? Listen to the commander, who orders what is right.

As comment upon this passage and its context we may quote Flew:

> There are few of the Christian writers of that age, or indeed of any age, who see with such clearness as Clement that the gift of communion with God brings with it not only a reinforcement of heavenly virtues, but also a transfiguration of the common task. Clement is depicting as an ideal a life that can be lived in Alexandria, near the Serapeum, amid a busy, commercial, pleasure-loving, and excitable population. And he can show that there is a Christian way of life, a grace and dignity of behaviour, that come as the natural fruit of the new relationship with God. This new way of life is apparent throughout the pages of the *Paedagogus*, or *Instructor*, the second of his great treatises. But rarely has the transformation of the work

[1] Edwyn Bevan, *Christianity*, (Home University Library,) pp. 129-131.
[2] *Protrepticus* (Chap. X). (Ante-Nicene Christian Library,) Vol. IV, p. 92.

of life been sung more harmoniously than in the famous passage of the *Protrepticus* (Chap. X).[1]

and further:

> At first sight it seems that Clement's doctrine of the two lives, which he draws from Philo, rests on a difference between faith and knowledge; and that the lower life of the ordinary believer is a life of faith, while the higher life, that of the Christian Gnostic, is a life of knowledge. Dr. Bigg has given the weight of his authority to this interpretation (*Christian Platonists*, 2nd edn., 1913, pp. 121, 124, 126). But there are reasons for questioning this view.
>
> The practical problem which lay before Clement must first be stated. Crowds were pressing into the Christian Church; the level of moral attainment was low, and their faith elementary. They were bringing with them many pagan prejudices, and the moral taint of the past still lingered about them. Such believers needed discipline and instruction. Clement has essayed that task in his *Paedagogus*. But in addition to these, and perhaps even among them, there were other enquirers after truth, who could not be content with spiritual mediocrity, and who hungered after a richer experience of God. Every minister of a church who understands his people knows that such a group exists, and often he has words which he speaks to them alone. To such an inner circle Clement addressed his *Stromata* "From the premises of his own intellectual mysticism, the greater knowledge of God to which they aspired involved not only a better comprehension, but also a more complete assimilation of the divine life, so that these gnostics in achieving their goal would become a kind of divine aristocracy."[2]

The *Protrepticus* was written before 189 A.D. and may be taken as occupying a mid position between *Ad Diognetum* and Eusebius. The writer's predicament was precisely the same as that of Eusebius, namely how to present practicable ethical demands to the half-converted. Yet Clement retains more of the enthusiasm and idealism of *Ad Diognetum*, and does not yet accept the "two distinct characters" of the

[1] Flew, *The Idea of Perfection*, p. 139.
[2] *Ibid.*, p. 140. Last sentence quoted from Casey, *Harvard Theol. Review*, xviii, 71.

Christian life. Clement stood between the Gnostics, to whom perfection lay in separation from the world (so that Gnostic beliefs were one of the contributing causes of monasticism), and those who desired a definition of the minimum in belief and conduct that would allow masses of men to call themselves Christian. Both the maximum and the minimum needed to be defined, the ideal of perfection and the first steps in discipleship. But unfortunately the latter degenerated into the conditions of conformity by the unconverted and the half-converted, who had no intention of doing more than barely sufficient to "satisfy the examiners".

If this distinction "saved Christianity", as Bishop Kirk says, it did so at a terrible price in creating a distinction between sacred and secular, *as if they were different kinds of life*, "that the Christian life is of two distinct characters". As a result, on the Roman view the true "vocation" has been the call to the monastery or the ministry, and Rome till lately has had no satisfactory doctrine of secular vocation.[1] Further, the monk, the nun and the priest, being the only people who really could have a sense of vocation, had a position of religious privilege as over against the laity, who in lacking such spiritual security and purpose became entirely dependent upon the mediation of those with such a vocation.

The thing to note here particularly, besides the full-fledged recognition of the two standards, is that the "mobilized" morality of New Testament times, in urgent expectation of an immediate crisis of judgment, has been standardized, and elevated into the "absolute" ethic of the monastic life in its three dimensions of poverty, celibacy and non-resistance (or absolute obedience); while life "in the world" is relegated to the standing of a second-rate kind of morality, cut off from the best. Two things seem to have been confused, the view that there are *different degrees of progress in the Christian life*, and the view that there are *two distinct kinds of Christian life*. The preference Greek philosophy showed for the contem-

[1] Cf. Fanfani, *Catholicism, Protestantism and Capitalism*, p. 204, etc.

plative as against the active life led to the hardening of the distinction, till we reach the view characteristic of (though not unchallenged within) the Roman Church till the Reformation, that the true and typical Christian life and "religious vocation" was confined within the walls of a monastery. All outside was "secular". The ascetic alone had a "vocation" to aim at perfection. The householder and man of affairs was fortunate if his "avocation" did not lead him to miss salvation. It is true there were many in every period, notably St. Thomas Aquinas himself, who struggled against this false antithesis between sacred and secular, and tried with more or less success to emphasize the truly heroic qualities of the Christian life lived in the world yet not of it. Like a singularly bright light shining in great darkness we have the example of St. Francis of Assisi. But to this day to the ordinary Roman Catholic, the "religious vocation", "vocation" and even "religion", are freely used as if they were appropriate only to "the religious", the monk, the nun, and the cleric. Life "in the world", in the family, and in affairs, disqualifies from the true and typical spiritual life.[1]

It is not possible here to do more than refer to the subsequent history of the two standards in Christian morality. Bishop Kirk, in his *Vision of God*,[2] draws a distinction between a valid form and an invalid form. There *are* different stages and degrees of perfection in the Christian life, but it can never be right to choose deliberately the unheroic course, contenting ourselves with the minimum and refusing to acknowledge the claims of the highest to an absolute obedience. Nor can it be right to debar the great masses of mankind by reason of the necessities of their life in the workaday world and in their homes, from the possibility of attaining to a perfection reserved only for the celibate living in a monastery. Bishop Kirk examines a wealth of evidence from

[1] "I describe the religious vocation from the point of view of one who had no such vocation." Monica Baldwin, *I Leap Over the Wall*, p. 8, of her withdrawal from life in a convent.

[2] *Op. cit.*, pp. 242-57 and 517-34.

the early and medieval writers to show how difficult the problem was and how in the end the view we have seen in Eusebius won the day and the whole legalist paraphernalia of works of supererogation, etc., and the *thesaurus meritorum* prepared for and made inevitable the revolution of the Reformation, when Luther, Calvin and others tried to return to New Testament simplicity.

The doctrine of Christian perfection depends a good deal upon the exegesis of certain texts and the meaning in particular of the Greek word *teleios*. It cannot be maintained that the Reformation solved the problem by accepting the highest attainments of Christian perfection as the privilege and duty of everyone, instead of the exclusive prerogative of a spiritual *élite*.

We have surely seen enough in the history of the Church to convince us that Pentecost is or should be for everybody, and yet that the ecstasies of Pentecost are not for every day. The sectary is right in claiming that perfection and nothing less is the purpose of God for every redeemed soul, but wrong in identifying that perfection with a daily dwelling on the Mountain of Transfiguration. Indeed it is an interesting study in vocation to note how the Mountain of Transfiguration was for the three alone with Jesus, whereas Pentecost, we believe, was for all faithful disciples. Religion without ecstasy is religion without release and, therefore, without power, as we see it in Acts 19: 1–7. But ecstasy cannot be incarnated into our daily state, any more than the Sacrament can become daily bread. Perfection is not an emotional condition, but a quality of character. Married life is not all honeymoon, in fact it never is honeymoon again, but a growth in grace and in knowledge which has further mountain peaks of discovery and revelation always ahead. The decisive thing about Pentecost was not the temporary eccentricities, inevitable and important though these were, but the permanent spiritual and ethical transformation of the disciples who had now become centres of overwhelming spiritual power, or rather instruments of such power and so to speak incarnations of it.

As we shall see in a later chapter, the Protestant Ethic needs to make it quite clear that there is a difference between the vocation of some and the duty of everyone, though it rejects the two standards as still maintained by Rome. The Roman and Protestant doctrine (and practice) cannot be so easily reconciled as Edwyn Bevan imagined. The Roman teaching remains aristocratic, exalting contemplation above action where the Protestant view, under the influence of Kant, has become too equalitarian without sufficient provision for the differentiation of duty. But it is difficult to justify the contention of Canon Hannay:

> It is to be observed that the Protestant theologian's denial of special honour to lives of complete renunciation has had a certain effect. Protestantism is less rich than Catholicism in examples of heroic Christianity. The general tendency of Protestantism has been to raise to a high level the common Christian life and to develop certain virtues of a kind suitable to the lives of citizens. It has not made for, and, except in comparatively rare instances, has not achieved, the production of unique saints, like, for example, St. Francis of Assisi, whose devotion lays hold upon the popular imagination. This failure must be attributed to the denial of the doctrine of "counsels" and "precepts", and the consequent unwillingness of Protestant teachers to hold up for admiration lives which must always be rare, and are never imitable, except by those who realize the peculiar glory of very great kinds of renunciation.[1]

Hannay in his article merits Kirk's criticism that he fails to distinguish between the valid and invalid forms of the double standard theory, but he goes on in the article to point out how "it has happened that certain evangelical sayings, regarded by the Schoolmen as counsels of perfection [and therefore not the duty of everyone], have, in times of high religious vitality, laid hold of the consciences of earnest Protestants and compelled obedience". Hence the Quakers,

---

[1] In *E.R.E.*, Vol. IV, p. 205 a, article on "Counsels and Precepts".

making of pacifism a "precept" obligatory on all, had to separate from a Church which did not so believe, and so this inability to differentiate between "counsels of perfection" and commands laid upon every Christian lies at the root of the fissiparous tendency of Protestantism. We shall return to this problem later, and examine the contention that Protestantism in repudiating the absolute monastic ethic had inevitably to accept a sectarian ethic to provide for the moral heroism of individuals and groups with a special vocation. We shall postpone also to Part II quotations from Calvin and Luther in which they repudiated the two-standards doctrine in favour of a vocational doctrine of the supreme spiritual importance of dedicated daily life, as lived in the family and market-place.

It is interesting that in our day, Lord Lindsay, with almost incredible *naïveté* has attempted a new version of the two standards in his *The Two Moralities*. After distinguishing the morality of "My Station and its Duties" from the morality of grace or the challenge to perfection, as if these could be defined over against each other as completely antithetical, in his conclusion he maintains that "there is no conflict here between the two moralities, though there is a contrast".[1] This book shows well how difficult it is for one brought up in the later Hegelian school to develop a truly Christian ethic without introducing the principle of vocation, by which duty is differentiated and we escape from the pitfalls alike of utilitarianism and of legalism. There are not two moralities, there is but one—in its vertical aspect a morality of duty determined by the call of God, in any vocation, in its horizontal aspect a function of my station and its duties. As we shall see there is no contradiction between these different dimensions of duty. This leads us to our next chapter, on the Christian conscience.

[1] p. 98.

Note to Chapter Three

TROELTSCH, *The Social Teaching of the Christian Churches*, Vol. I, Chap. I, p. 121 (Geo. Allen & Unwin).

"The Early Church seems to have been familiar with the idea of variety in business and trade, and with differences of rank and class, but it had no idea of a 'calling', in the sense in which that word was used in the central period of the Middle Ages and by the early Protestants. The reason for this is obvious. An ethic which holds that the differences that do exist are due to sin, and which at its best regards the division of labour as a Divine arrangement adapted to the needs of fallen humanity, is inherently unable to see any value in 'callings' at all. At the beginning, during the period when the Church appealed mainly to the lower middle class, its eschatological outlook and the spirit of other-worldliness had also prevented the development of this feeling. At the outset the Jewish artisan point of view, the emphasis on the absolutism of the Divine Government of the world, as well as on predestination, had strongly emphasized the fact that external inequality could exist alongside of an interior equality, while at the same time work was held in high esteem. As the Church strengthened her position, however, more and more clearly religious equality stood out as an essentially attractive element in Christian doctrine; it became fused with the Stoic ideal of Reason, and it asserted that at least in the Primitive State entire equality had prevailed. This, however, had the effect of decreasing the social distinctions in the contemporary social order, although it did not remove them. On the other hand, however, the social order of the Imperial period did not provide a basis for the development of this conception; this was only given at a later stage by the feudal society of the Middle Ages, and then, above all, by the industrial town with its closely knit political and economic unity. Apart from the river-civilization of Egypt and Mesopotamia, the social life of the Imperial period was based upon the town with its democratic form of organization, upon the equal right of citizenship for all, upon a comparative freedom in trade and emigration (which, however, steadily decreased), upon differences in wealth and position, which determined the question of admission into the ranks of the upper classes, upon the industrial work of the lower classes, carried out by slaves or freedmen who were provisionally placed in charge; the latter were not permitted, however, to form independent municipal organizations similar to those which were afterwards developed by working men in the Middle Ages. The town still held the ideal of the 'private gentleman and capitalist', and this class was obliged to remain part of the city proletariat. Above all, this social order of the Ancient World was determined by the fact that it was predominantly a coastal civilization, which only created towns at its centres of organization for military and commercial reasons. The social order of the Middle Ages, on the other hand, was based upon a continental or inland civilization, which produced a vastly more intensive and more richly differentiated agrarian, and then industrial, civilization with a stable organization. Thus, in the early days, even from the point of view of Society itself, there existed no stimulus which might eventually give birth to the idea of a stable, well-organized system of 'callings' and of the division of labour. Until the time of Constantine all the leaders of the Church take this point of view; they regard all callings with complete indifference, as 'fate' or 'destiny', and they merely criticize them without attempting to make concrete constructive suggestions. From the third and fourth centuries onward, however, the social order of the Ancient World developed in the direction of settled organization; military and official positions became hereditary; compulsory associations of labourers were formed within the food-producing industries, and some of these corporations resembled the later institutions of feudal times. This development took place alongside of the gradual relapse into an economy based on agriculture, the growth of an inland civilization, the decrease in the value of money, and the State system of regulation which tried to grapple with these difficulties. It may be that this development gave rise to the idea which often appears in the writings of the Fathers of the fourth century—that is, of a necessary social organization which would be mutually complementary. This idea, however, was always entirely obliterated by their habit of harping upon the equality of the Primitive State, and their insistence on the restoration of equality by love and sacrifice, which, if it cannot be done in the world must be carried out in the monastic life. The increasing esteem in which monasticism was held was due to the very fact that it seemed impossible to regard this social order—with all its difficulty, friction, conflict, and reaction—as a system of 'callings' ordained by God and destined to contribute its part to the supreme religious meaning of life. On the other hand, we shall see that the Middle Ages only succeeded in fitting monasticism —that high explosive of all social systems—into its social order to the extent in which it made the monastic life one among several suitable 'callings'. Once this fact has been clearly perceived we have gained a very important clue to the understanding of the difference between primitive, mediæval, and modern Christianity.

"At first, under the influence of the eschatological outlook and the Pauline conservative attitude, the duty of the Christian was summed up in obedience to the exhortation, 'Let every man abide in the same calling wherein he was called' (1 Cor. vii, 20), in which he was to maintain the Christian virtues. Thus Christians took part in all the general conditions of life and industry, and avoided only those callings which were impossible for them as Christians; those who had lost their work for this reason were cared for by the Church. In those stern early days, however, this principle of excluding all unsuitable employments cut very deeply into life. All offices and callings were barred which had any connection with idol-worship, or with the worship of the Emperor, or those which had anything to do with bloodshed or with capital punishment, or those which would bring Christians into contact with pagan immorality. This meant that Christians were debarred from taking service under the State or the municipality; they could not serve as judges or as officers in the army; any kind of military service, indeed, was impossible. The drama, art, and rhetoric were also forbidden. At first, however, these restrictions did not affect the Early Church very harshly, owing to the class from which its members were drawn. It was far more deeply affected by the exclusion from all technical occupations, from all arts and crafts which had any connection with idolatrous emblems or with pagan-worship: 'carpenters, stucco-workers, cabinet-makers, thatchers, goldleaf-beaters, painters, workers in bronze, and engravers—all these are forbidden to take any part whatever in any work which is necessary for temple service.' That, of course, included all dealers in meat, flowers, and other things used in temple-worship. Magicians and astrologers are tabooed. A Christian could not be a school teacher nor a teacher of science, since those professions were connected with idolatry through the books they had to use and in other ways. The effect of all this on social life was very evident. The Christians were proud of this opposition between their way of life and that of paganism, and they laid stress on the fact that they were able to cause stagnation in trade. The pagans were aware of the danger; the famous report of Pliny emphasizes the economic desolation, and Celsus complains that if such principles prevail the Emperor will soon have no army and no officials, and that the Empire will perish. Origen's reply to this complaint is highly characteristic: 'If all Romans would accept the Faith they would conquer their enemies by prayer and supplication, or rather they would no longer have any enemies at all, for the Divine power would preserve them.' 'There is no one who fights better for the King than we. It is true that we do not go with him into battle, even when he desires it, but we fight for him by forming an army of our own, an army of piety, through our prayers to the Godhead.' 'Once all men have become Christians, then even the barbarians will be inclined towards peace.'

"In such a situation, of course, it is clear that the question of social reform could not arise. The Church had no idea that the Christian criticism of Society ought to lead to an organic reform. The leaders of the Church believed that God would prevent Society from going to pieces. From the Christian point of view it was sufficient to renounce the forbidden professions and occupations; the rest of the social order could go on as usual. Indeed, the Christians had already gained a position which entitled them to be regarded, in the opinion of the writer of the *Epistle to Diognetus*, as 'the soul' of the world'

.   .   .   .

"The dominant idea is not that of a 'calling', but of the lot which falls to each individual. The point on which most emphasis is laid is the 'admirable and well-known system of the organization of the Christian community'[1]"

Again we can gain an important insight into these tendencies without accepting all Troeltsch's sweeping generalizations.

[1] *Ad Diognetum*, 5, 4.

Chapter Four

CONSCIENCE, DUTY AND VOCATION

CONSCIENCE is not a peculiarly Christian phenomenon. There is only one occasion when the Greek word for conscience is used in the Gospels (John 8: 9), and then it is a doubtful reading with a disputed meaning On the other hand, the use of the word conscience in the Epistles is fairly frequent. The word is not used in the Old Testament, but the idea of conscious guilt is universal—e.g. the Fall, Cain and Abel, Joseph's brethren, and the classic instance of the 51st psalm. In the New Testament, although there is no word for conscience in the Gospels, the moral fact is prominent, for example in Matthew 6: 22-23, and Luke 11: 34— the inward eye of the soul and the light of the body.

It is only in revealed religion and in particular in the religion of the Old Testament, that the real sense of sin arises, with the belief in the holiness of God and realization that disobedience to such a God is a breach in the covenant relationship. There is no parallel to the 51st psalm in the whole of pagan literature. Conscience, therefore, becomes an almost totally new phenomenon, in the light of this realization of guilt in the presence of a Holy God, and in the light of our vocation from God. When we pass to the New Testament, we have again a transformation in conscience, for we have the further revelation of the love of God in the Incarnation, the Cross, the Resurrection and the Holy Spirit, one of whose primary functions is to bring the conviction of sin (John 16: 8–11). That is to say, the Christian conscience is or ought to be *sui generis:* and in fact a dispassionate view of history shows that this is so, and the extraordinary anomalies and perversions of the Christian conscience do no more to disprove its validity and its uniqueness than the highlights of the pagan conscience prove man to stand in no need of redemption.

It is a curious thing that in several languages the word for conscience is a collective word, implying a sense of another unseen, knowing presence, "con-science", German *Gewissen*, Greek *suneidesis*. It was the Stoics who seem to have invented this use of the word for an unseen witness or judge, but Socrates' *daimonion* is really a kind of conscience, and similarly in various forms it appears in Greek tragedy.

Conscience implies self-consciousness, the capacity to entertain ideas without identifying ourselves with them, of criticizing oneself. At the animal level below self-consciousness, conscience strictly speaking is impossible. In the relations of shame, pity and reverence (as in Solovyof), where we have human conditions, we can speak of a universal moral consciousness, and conscience is possible as a power of making moral judgments. We may say that the moral conscience is universal where a mentality can be described as human. All human beings have some power of distinguishing between good and evil, right and wrong. The whole history of ethics may be held to be an inquiry into the nature of conscience. Without entering into that age-long discussion, we may say first that there is an element of objectivity required. That is to say, conscience must indicate real moral values and distinctions. "Without objectivity ethic has no meaning" (von Hartmann). But, on the other hand, the growth and development and diversity of conscience are beyond dispute. "No individual can make a conscience for himself. He always needs a society to make it for him" (T. H. Green). In conscience there is then (*a*) a constant, and so it may be held to be the "stern daughter of the voice of God", and also (*b*) a variable, which is a "function" of character and circumstances—"Wisdom dealt with mortal powers". Observe how this double or dialectical nature of conscience is simply a recurrence in another medium of the fundamental problems of theology, revelation and faith, grace and personality, eternity and time, the two "natures" in the person of Christ, and the dialectical nature of the Church as a divine ordinance and a human institution.

Note further that conscience in its universal character does not indicate the supreme good for man, but enables a man to distinguish between right and wrong at an actual time and situation. The time and situation then largely determine the nature of its judgment, and *the variations of conscience* are no objections to its authority, but *are an evidence of its practical moral worth*. It deals with "my station and its duties" and does not reveal abstract, ultimate moral values or principles, except indirectly.

Is conscience infallible? Do we mean subjectively infallible —that is to say, that it is always right for me to obey my conscience?—or objectively infallible?—that is, it never makes mistakes? We must admit that many grave errors, crimes and sins have been performed in the name of conscience, many of them with the best intentions. That is to say, conscience is educable, and there is an element of progress involved in it—e.g. polygamy in the Old Testament, slavery until modern times.

What is the distinctive thing about the Christian conscience? The answer is that faith and the assurance of faith make a Christian conscience.[1]

For example, Luther's attitude at Worms was not merely the beginning of a new era in Christian faith, but the beginning of a new era of the Christian conscience. "Unless I be convinced by Scripture and reason, I neither can nor dare

[1] "Luther, with his fine linguistic sense, has also spoken of faith and the assurance of faith as the Christian conscience, in order to indicate that the immediate certainty of faith is not merely for a subjective, but of a subjective-objective kind." Dorner, *System of Christian Ethics*, p. 231.

retract anything, for my conscience is a captive to God's word, and it is neither safe nor right to go against conscience. There I take my stand. I can do no otherwise. So help me God." Note here the two (objective) standards to which Luther appeals: (1) God's word and (2) reason. Luther confronted alone the civil and ecclesiastical power of his time, but not as an eccentric individualist. Perhaps this Reformation-Renaissance era has now run into excessive individualism, but Luther, Calvin and the Reformers generally were fully conscious of the importance of a Church fellowship, even while they resisted the ecclesiastical institution that claimed to represent, possess and exercise all the functions and prerogatives of the Church fellowship.

The new era, with its autonomy of the responsible conscience of the believer, did not inaugurate the Christian conscience, though we Protestants believe that in it the Christian conscience came into its own, and so to speak emerged from the long tutelage of earlier ages. Christian faith from the start showed itself in a new sensitiveness of conscience, and wherever Christian faith appears new qualities of conscience accompany it inevitably, just because faith is vision by sinful man of a holy God.

"The influence of faith by which the conscience becomes Christian, will produce two marked effects in the moral consciousness: it will greatly intensify the sense of personal responsibility, and it will also light up conscientiousness with a sense of freedom. The touch of the Spirit of Christ awakens conscience to a sense of the whole obligation of a human life before unrealized. The effect of conversion on the natural conscience is to raise it to a higher power."[1] In other words a new dimension is added to conscience by conversion. St. Paul is wrestling with this problem especially in Romans 2 and 7.

Without entering into the perennial controversy as regards the distinction and relationship between faith and rea-

[1] Newman Smyth, *Christian Ethics*, pp. 293, 294.

son, we may claim that the Christian conscience, unlike the Kantian conscience, is more than an embodied reason, though Luther appealed to reason when appealing to Scripture. Faith is nothing if not individual, in fact it is a personal, or, if you like, supra-personal relationship, which cannot be defined or completely described in rational terms. Hence, as faith transforms the human personality until it becomes progressively endowed with the wisdom, love and power of Christ, so by the same process and inevitably, the conscience comes to approximate more and more to that of Christ with His sensitiveness to the distinction between right and wrong and His sure tread in the midst of temptation. "It is distinctive of the Christian life, that while it grows more conscientious, it also grows less and less a task of duty and more and more a service of delight. The Christian faith renders life throughout a fulfilment of a trust. By faith the law of love is transformed into the love of law."[1] The Christian conscience then should be more and more perfectly the mind of Christ in us. Conscience is not a way or another way of knowing things. It is no mere practical syllogism, as Aristotle maintained, but an expression of the whole character, and its "magisterial and manifest authority" (Butler) comes from its representative nature. It represents the wholeness of man in the ideal sense, as against the urgency of any particular appetite or impulse. Luther, in claiming autonomy of faith from ecclesiastical dictation, inevitably claimed also autonomy of conscience; and the Protestant freedom, as a form of religious experience far more diversified and complex than any dictated or externally dominated experience can be, results not merely in distinctive doctrine, but in a distinctive ethic.

If faith and conscience are to the Christian simply different versions of one attitude, then Christian duty will be determined by this faith-conscience relationship—such a relationship inevitably involving not merely a link of the

[1] Newman Smyth, *ibid.*, p. 294.

soul with God, but a corresponding link of the soul with its fellows. Hence Luther, standing with a Bible in his hand and confronting the authorities in Church and State on the strength of the Word of God, as revealed in Scripture, is a symbol of distinctive elements in the development of the Christian conscience ever since.

The trouble is that Kant, and not Luther and Calvin, has been adopted too widely as the prophet of the Christian conscience, so that most recent thinking on the subject has been philosophical and, so to speak, *a priori*. From the pulpit it has been proclaimed as Gospel that duty is categorical, absolute and universal, whereas in the pew the worshippers and believers knew that each had for himself to steer a precarious way amid the pitfalls and halflights of a devious pilgrimage, compassed about with the relativities of history. Rome has never made any secret of its distinction between the absolute ethic, as practised in the sheltered seclusion of the monastery, with its three dimensions of celibacy, poverty and passive obedience, and the relative ethic, which was all that in secular life plain men and women could aspire to. The religious life to which men received a call was shut off from affairs, and in affairs the absolute had to be modified and accommodated into a relative ethic of compromise and a measure of uncertainty. Matthew 19, on the Roman exegesis, gives validity to the distinction between the two kinds of life, the one of which aims at perfection and the other is content to be allowed to enter the Kingdom on keeping the commandments. The Romans accuse us Protestants, not without some reason, of preaching perfectionism and practicing secular compromise.

We have now also to reckon with the influence of the concept of evolution upon all our thinking and our practice. The result has been widespread relativity in ethics and, with the banishing or neglect of the element of supernatural sanction, an ethic of pure expediency in its utilitarian or other forms has become widespread. To it there are no absolutes.

"Man is the measure of all things." It is one of the most obvious and distressing gulfs between pulpit and pew that the pulpit declares a Kantian, absolutist, metaphysical ethic and the pew practises an evolutionary, opportunist, economic ethic. We have to realize that there is an element of relativity about duty. Duty may be absolute in the sense that I must obey my conscience at all costs, in all places and at all times; but that does not entitle me to turn to my neighbour and say that what my conscience bids me do, he also must do, and that both of us must hold to precisely the same line at all times and in all circumstances. *Duty may be absolute without being universal, and the vocation of some need not necessarily be the duty of all.* We have to recognize that "my station and its duties" does to some extent determine what my conduct should be, and that our behaviour is not *in vacuo*. Here is where the principle of vocation may rescue the Protestant ethic from its deification of Kant. We no longer maintain in doctrine that any church or any individual has or can have a monopoly of truth. Each bears testimony to the versions or perspectives of truth granted to him. Darwin, Freud, Marx, and Mannheim all press home upon us the element of relativity that affects all our judgments, our beliefs and our actions, none of which ever takes place *in vacuo*. We do not need to accept Marx or Freud or any of the others at their face value, but the cumulative effect of their thinking on the moral and intellectual climate of our time is to make a Kantian absolutism in thought or practice no longer possible.

"In the historic world there are no ideals, but only facts— no truths, but only facts. There is no reason, no honesty, no equity, no final aim, but only facts. . . . In the real world there are no states built according to ideals, but only states that have *grown*, and these are nothing but living peoples 'in form'."[1]

If we accept this interpretation of history we must abandon our Christian faith. But against a certain kind of abstract

[1] Spengler, *The Decline of the West, II,* p. 368.

idealism Spengler's criticism, like Marx's, has a measure of justification, for such idealism is based upon illusions about human nature and human destiny.

This does not mean that we are to believe that we are purely creatures of our time, which would mean also victims of our circumstances; but it does mean that we have to think of ourselves and our duty as real persons, acting in real places upon real conditions. We do not believe that all idealism is illusion, nor that a materialistic realism is the necessary interpretation of the world; but Christian realism in action requires of us an articulation of duty, broken down into the actual situations in which men find themselves. Confronted with a Kantian absolutism on the one hand and an evolutionary relativism on the other, we have in the doctrine of vocation the means to our hand of finding a course which is neither of these and better than either—namely—the Christian conscience enlightened (and convicted) by the Holy Spirit in the fellowship of the Church, which tells me what to do here and now. We are neither abstract idealists nor unprincipled opportunists, but if we believe that God speaks to real persons in guidance and warning, we must believe that the Christian conscience is the voice of God, determining my duty here and now.

Duty is relative, but relative to vocation, not, if one may use the phrase, absolutely relative. The idea of absolute obligation cannot be imposed by anyone upon himself, but if we accept the Gospel teaching about God and Jesus and ourselves and the classical interpretation of that teaching in St. Paul, we see that there is a certain measure of flexibility in our actual conduct along with an absolute devotion to our Lord. We notice in St. Paul, for instance (1 Cor. 10: 26, 28) how apparently contradictory courses may be called for in closely similar circumstances, as applications or interpretations of the same principle.

The application of this to ordinary, everyday life and to the proclamation of the Word of God from the pulpit, looks obvious but is far from easy, and is one of the questions most troubling us to-day. How far should the pulpit confine itself to the proclamation of truth in general terms, how far should it condescend upon particulars, enunciate *principia media* and deal with actual cases of conscience? The Roman Church has its elaborate casuistry, but no Protestant minister who is proclaiming the Gospel can escape from the duty of giving guidance in cases of conscience, in many of which an absolutely and abstractly right course of action may seem to be impossible. There has not been since Richard Baxter's *Directory* and *The New Whole Duty of Man* any serious attempt at a Protestant system of casuistry in English, and indeed any such system of legalistic attitudes or any codification of duties is quite repugnant to our Protestant faith and way of life.

Here the particular value of Scripture is very obvious, although it is the despair of the system-monger and the person who wants a code. Scripture almost invariably deals with particular persons, and principles only as incorporated or incarnated in particular instances. The *Logos* is always being made flesh. In working out a doctrine of vocation to suit our age, its apparently endless relativity and its apparently irrelevant absolutes, we are facing again the problem of incarnation which confronts us also in the Church as it struggles to incorporate in a human institution the incommensurable values of the spirit. However difficult it may be, it is only in the Christian fellowship and through it that the Christian conscience will gain any clear guidance, even from Scripture, to permit the troubled soul to pick its way through the world.

Confronted, as we are, with varying solutions of the problem how to determine our Christian duty, we reject Kantian *a priori* inflexibility, and at the other extreme, a utilitarian ethic of mere opportunism, economic or other, and also the Roman method of casuistical legalism, in favour of a vocational ethic, where duty is broken down into terms of our actual situation without losing sight of the absolutes. On this view the variations of conscience are like the variations of a compass, supremely important and responsive to objective stable influences, not incalculable like the variations of a weathercock, which indicate only the direction in which the wind happens to be blowing at the moment, though this, too, has its cosmic significance. The Kantian conscience is like a compass clamped to indicate magnetic north, *where we are*, but unable to offer any guidance the moment we begin to move. The utilitarian conscience is like the weathercock, telling only the favourable wind at the moment. No codification or classification of virtues, duties, and their corresponding vices and lapses, interpreted by the skilled expert in the cure of souls by casuistical methods, can compare with the almost instinctive and intuitive conviction of the soul walking in daily converse with Jesus and in the fellowship of the Church. Here he will find the antidote to individualism in its loneliness and insecurity and its tendency to fanaticism when left to itself, without the constant reminder that its own perspectives of truth and duty are only contributory features of one objective world of real values, which individuals must learn to recognize and discover. In such a soul absolutes are effective in the actual situations of daily life. The man or woman with a vocation derived from a vision of God may have very imperfect views of the nature of his beliefs and his duty, but however inarticulate he may be, his daily intercourse with, and confrontation by the living Christ through the Holy Spirit will keep his conscience sensitive to right and wrong, and his faith progressively free from error. The intuitive faith and conscience of such a person provide the compass for daily living which theology and ethics may criticize and explain, but cannot gainsay or disobey:—

The rest may reason and welcome: 'tis we musicians know.

Chapter Five

LIVING as we do in an age that is shadowed by sinister clouds of imminent war, while we still have fresh in our memories the happenings and sufferings of two other wars, we long for one clear and convincing Word of God for our guidance in this dominant ethical problem of our day. Yet on no other question, except possibly the Sacraments, is Christian thought more divided.

My own memory goes still, farther back to the time when as a boy I would get up early to read the latest news about the Boer War in the morning paper before going to school. How remote it was, though exciting enough to a boy! No one belonging to me was engaged in it, it made no difference to my life except to provide me with popular idols for hero worship and engrossing tales of courage and danger. I can vividly remember how remote even the beginnings in 1914 were to a student, till suddenly with the first reverses and recruiting appeals I realized "This means you". Nineteen-thirty-nine and even more 1940 shattered whatever ivory towers still survived in our land, and now the atom bomb and promise of the hydrogen bomb seem to complete the obliteration of the non-combatant, and the elimination of neutrality. So much earnest Christian idealism had devoted itself to an attempt to limit the cruelty and destructiveness of war, to define and safeguard the status of non-combatants, to humanize the treatment of prisoners, etc., that it took a

67

long time for decent people to realize the meaning of total war, unless they were actually exposed to the Blitz. Even now the difficulty that Church representatives have in getting agreement on any statement about atomic warfare should warn us of the complexity of the ethical issues involved.

But rude experience has prised us loose from the complacent opinion—it was scarcely a conviction—that peace is the natural, normal and easy relationship among nations, while war is unnatural, abnormal, episodic and incidental. Human history contains far more and possibly even more important things than war, and the writing of history has perhaps in the past been too exclusively a recital of wars and rumours of wars. Peace is the exception, war more nearly the rule than "Victorian optimism" was willing to admit. We may no longer say with Bagehot that wars "are by their incessant fractures of old images, and by their constant infusion of new elements, the real regenerators of society",[1] that "the conflict of nations is at first a main force in the improvement of nations",[2] or that "it is wars that make nations".[3] Ever since the discovery of gunpowder war has ceased to be a eugenic agent in history, and each new discovery has made it more dysgenic. As Rousseau saw, "War is constituted by a relation between things, and not between persons".[4] The worst wickedness of war is that it treats persons as things and makes people treat one another as things. That is why modern war is so devastatingly demoralizing, and the more mechanical it becomes the more immoral it must be.

Even if we believe war to be an anachronism, we are no nearer getting rid of it, as one can get rid of the appendix, which is also an anachronism. Nothing has yet been devised to take the place of war in human history and provide "a moral equivalent" for it.

We cannot afford to ignore the fact that certain features of our national and international relationships may at any time

[1] *Physics and Politics*, (1872) p. 144. [2] *Op. cit.* p. 83.
[3] *Op. cit.*, p. 77. [4] *The Social Contract*, I, Chap. iv.

go bad on us, and even if simply let alone will promote war almost automatically. Anachronisms are always dangerous. "The price of peace is eternal vigilance." Commercial competition, proclaimed by the Manchester School as the moral equivalent of war, turns out instead to be a powerful agency in promoting war, particularly when markets are shrinking.

The new identification, or at any rate correlation, of the political and the economic in the totalitarian and to a lesser extent in the welfare state, accentuates the problem by extending the sphere of "legitimate interests" and erecting more of them into "vital interests", in which the honour of a whole nation may be engaged, as well as the welfare of a section of its citizens. "It is not improbable that mistakes as to national vocation have been principal causes of devastating wars."[1] It is when patriotism assumes the "supernatural sanction" of religion that an explosive mixture appears leading almost inevitably to war. As Lord Eustace Percy with rare insight has seen: "Those who appeal to force for the limited ends of mere social order can limit their use of it—not so the man who appeals to it as an instrument of perfection."[2] This principle has its application both (a) to such a situation as that of the pseudo-religions such as fascism and communism, as they erect their own material idealisms into a religion, or attempt to enlist religion to secure, on behalf of the duties of citizenship, the motives and sacrifice called out by patriotism in war; and (b) to the situation in the anti-communist countries, where pressure is put on the Church or churches to sublimate the political, economic and military struggle against communism to the level of a Crusade. Every war of the future will be a war of religion, for no country will go to war till it can give its cause the colour of a Crusade and so secure for its maintenance absolute loyalty of a heroic quality in the whole population. Nothing less can bring victory in total war.

The peculiar danger of our present situation arises from

[1] Lord, *Principles of Politics*, p. 304.   [2] *John Knox*, p. 289.

the fact that our capital-labour set-up till now seems to need war to make it function at its maximum efficiency; and economically it seems to need rapid and effective destruction to make production with full employment possible. It is only when geared up to war purposes that it overcomes certain inherent defects in the supply-demand economy. The Marshall Plan is in a sense a vindication of the Social Credit theory. Whether this defect is merely incidental and the credit-production system can be made to function normally without war pressures and demands, or whether the defect is inherent in and essential to all capitalist and democratic political economic structures, the future alone will show. The new welfare state is attempting to eliminate unemployment and also to eliminate the gravitation of our unregulated economic system towards war. It is only fair to note, though it increases the danger of our immediate situation, that even if our politico-economic situation has an economic urge towards war, the Soviet politico-economic situation has an even greater psychological urge towards war, to maintain the social solidarity the political structures require. The "purge" may begin by being party, it must inevitably proceed to be national and international. A Stalin must have a Tito; possibly a Soviet Russia must have a Korea.

We are confronted on every hand with a new situation, and in face of this situation the Church cannot apparently proclaim with unanimity one line of action or one governing principle or word of God. Even when in the past it has approached some common mind, it has been in support of an institution or method that we see now to have been inadequate for its purpose, and the complete loyalty inculcated by the Church was not always wise. We do not look back on the recruiting appeals and patriotic pulpits of 1914, nor on the Church support of the League of Nations between the wars, with unmitigated satisfaction. But confronted with the new totalitarianisms and the problems of total war, the Church cannot attempt to avoid the mistakes of the past by a noncommittal neutrality or even a non-combatant attitude. The character of war has changed, the efforts to humanize war have failed, the whole future of Christian civilization seems at stake. Never was there more need of clear, unequivocal guidance from the Church, and never was the Church less able to speak with one voice. The reasons for this are difficult to understand, and even more difficult to explain to many who in their predicament expect a message of salvation on the human plane for the tragedy now well over the horizon. How does our argument about vocation help us here? We must go back a little both logically and historically, to pick up the threads.

In the argument of the last chapter we maintained that truth, goodness, and beauty are objective; that is, we do not make them what they are by wishful thinking. There is a real hierarchy of moral values, more real in its way than the objective world in space. But we finite creatures have only subjective "versions" or "perspectives" of these objective values. None of us is in possession of the whole truth, none can peremptorily say that because this is right for me it is inevitably right for everyone, or even always right for myself. There is an element of subjectivity, of relativity, in all our moral judgments. But conscience when quickened by faith swings like a compass, never like a weathercock. It obeys, not my will, but some external voice applying to my immediate situation and indicating my duty in it. But just because these subjective changeable factors have to be taken into account, while it can never be right to act against my conscience, an ignorant or misguided conscience may make woeful mistakes.

That is why neither in philosophy nor in religion do we think that when we have said "conscience" we have said the last word. A selfish man persisting in his selfishness need not expect his conscience automatically to swing true to indicate right and wrong; it will be as much disturbed by his cherished selfishness as a compass by a large mass of magnetic steel placed close to it. Such a man's conscience will come to point to himself instead of to God—the worst form of idolatry. We must be prepared not merely to give a reasonable justification for the judgments of conscience (which is implied in the fact that they *are* judgments, though not necessarily consciously so, and not mere feelings or emotions), but to relate such decisions of conscience to what we believe of the character of God. Conscience is not an exclusively Christian phenomenon, as both Socrates and Paul witness, but the Christian conscience *is* a distinctive thing.

Something happens to the conscience of a man who is living in fellowship with God by faith, just as Paul said the conscience of a Christian differed both from the conscience of the Jew and from the conscience of the Gentile. But, if we press this further, we find Paul laying down that Christians within one church may feel called to give different testimony about certain matters of conduct. For example, in Romans, chapters 13, 14, and 15, and 1 Corinthians, chapter 10, we find him discussing questions of submission to civil magistrates, observance of days, the eating of meat, especially meat previously offered to idols, idolatry, fornication, and circumcision. In some cases no compromise or difference of opinion was permissible; in others "charity" should allow such difference; in still other cases a sense of corporate responsibility would lead to the strong denying themselves things perfectly harmless to them, but dangerous to the weak. No one could imagine St. Paul counselling the Church to regard idolatry, or impurity, or lying, as forms of behaviour permissible within the Church. But there was to be room as we would say within the one communion for a variety of opinion and testimony as of gifts,[1] so long as these were all honestly held up before Christ for His scrutiny, and held together by the bond of unity. The Church was the people who cared. Christ, as von Hügel was fond of saying, taught us to care. The Church is the fellowship of people who

[1] See, on this, Romans, Chap. 12.

have learnt to care for one another and for all mankind because of what Jesus did and does for us all.

What has all this got to do with pacifism? Much every way. There is now within every Church a body of people committed to more or less absolute pacifism, based on the Sermon on the Mount and other teachings of Jesus, a reading of history, and an attitude to the present predicament of mankind. In some cases they have been branded with heresy, and accused of disloyalty to their Church and their country, and have responded by accusing the Church which will not identify itself with them of apostasy and disloyalty to the teachings of our Lord. As Niebuhr says, there is a kind of pacifism much in evidence which *is* heretical, based on the humanitarian liberal belief in the perfectibility and sweet reasonableness of human nature, derived from the Renaissance and not from the Bible.[1] We saw this often in the claims made before the Tribunals for conscientious objectors, where it was sometimes maintained that education, persuasion, and a change of economic and political system will surmount all difficulties and banish all our ills, and rid us of this element of conflict in human affairs. We have not yet outgrown all our Crystal Palace Utopias.

Pacifism which is based on a naïve belief in the sweet reasonableness of human nature *is* a heresy. So Butterfield says of a certain ambassador: "Such an attitude to morality—such a neglect of a whole tradition of maxims in regard to this question—was not Christian in any sense of the word but belongs to a heresy black as the old Manichaean heresy. It is like the Bishop who said that if we totally disarmed he had too high an opinion of human nature to think that anybody would attack us. There might be great virtue in disarming and consenting to be made martyrs for the sake of the good cause; but to promise that we should not have to endure martyrdom in that situation, or to rely on such a supposition, is against both theology and history. It is essen-

[1] Reinhold Niebuhr, *Why the Christian Church is not Pacifist*, pp. 12-15.

tial not to have faith in human nature. Such faith is a recent heresy and a very disasterous one."[1]

True Christian pacifism, however, is based on the recognition that the distinctive and typical Christian attitude to evil is not resistance, but suffering, willingly undergone on behalf of others. Elements within the Church have realized this all through the ages of our Christian era, for it is a fundamental principle of the Gospel. We have seen the beginnings of the absolute ethic within the New Testament and traced it to its most extreme and permanent form in the monastic system. We Protestants believe that the "two standards" doctrine on which the monastic system was based is a perversion of the original Gospel, which set the ideal of perfection before all men; but the Church in all ages has had to choose: (1) to push out this kind of testimony; (2) to find room for it within the Church; or (3) to identify itself with it.

While certain early Christian writers have been responsible for pacifist utterances, notably Origen, Tertullian, and Lactantius (curiously enough all of them suspected or convicted of heresy on other grounds), the Early Church as a whole was never committed to a pacifist reading of the teaching of Jesus, e.g. "Resist not evil" (Matt. 5: 39). The view now fairly common that before Constantine the Church was pacifist, but after him it was too closely allied to the State to maintain such an attitude is simply not in accordance with the facts. From the very start the application of the principles of the Gospel to the pagan civil community round about it caused much difficulty, as was inevitable. If the Church's refusal to identify itself with pacifism is apostasy, it was led into apostasy not by Constantine, but by St. Paul (see Romans 13). The Christian conscience was troubled by the violence, corruption and idolatry inevitable in the soldier's life, but it was also troubled by the holding of property, the need for recourse to the law courts, and a thousand and one

---

[1] Herbert Butterfield, *Christianity and History*, pp. 46, 47.

problems, so troubled that, as we have seen, the most sensitive consciences sought escape in monasticism. The knight and the monk could both claim to be Christian, though the one had to fight, while the other could not, but had to pray. None of us can pretend we have reached a satisfactory and final solution of the problem how to relate the "evangelical simplicity" and the "love-perfectionism" of the Sermon on the Mount to the rough-and-tumble conflicts of our daily life in the world. The problem of the "absolute" and the "relative" ethic confronts us still, and nowhere more acutely than here.[1]

The pacifist case looks simple. We have the quintessence of the Gospel in the Sermon on the Mount. The Church is the Body of Christ, committed to take His way without compromise, and to offer itself for the sacrifice of the Cross, unwilling to lend its countenance to any of the partial rights and imperfect loyalties of this unfinished world. The crucifixion of the Church will redeem the world from violence. Pathetically, where this attitude has commended itself, numbers of the most earnest people have withdrawn from all association with bodies which were doing a great service to the community, such as the League of Nations Union in the period between the wars, and have impoverished by dividing the forces working for peace. Similarly, for better or for worse, in the early ages the moral earnestness that filled the monasteries was withdrawn from the tasks and problems of citizenship.

No system of collective security can be established on pacifist principles either within the State or among the nations; but, more fundamental even than that, the principle

[1] See the admirable surveys of the evidence on both sides in Hastings' *Dictionary of the Apostolic Church* (H.D.A.C.), Vol. 2, pp. 646b-673a (James Moffatt), and the *Encyclopaedia of Religion and Ethics* (E.R.E.), Vol. 12, pp. 675a-691b, also C. J. Cadoux, *The Early Christian Attitude to War, passim*, and his later book, *The Early Church and the World*, pp. 402-42. Although Cadoux was a pacifist, he was singularly fair in recording both sides, and much less sweeping in generalization than Troeltsch in the passage quoted on pp. 54, 56.

of the stewardship of the strong for the weak and of men and bodies for one another goes by the board. That is why many who are willing to acknowledge that Christianity has taught the world to care for liberty and justice, and men to care for one another, are bewildered when, in the name of Christ a Gospel is proclaimed which means acquiescence in the martyrdom of whole peoples, as, for instance, in the enslavement of the Chinese people by drugs under Japanese "protection", and in unspeakable horrors let loose in bestial cruelty in the so-called civilized world under the influence of the new ideologies. To our amazement we discover that the submission of one people to another, without a champion or a friend, far from arousing pity and chivalry, arouses sadism so terrible that we despair of ever cleansing the world from the brutalities that pollute it. It is a curious thing that, with a few exceptions, pacifism flourishes best in lands more or less remote from the actual horrors of war. The Quakers, notable exceptions to this, have been enabled to give their testimony and carry on their humanitarian work because they are protected in their persons, their property, and their Christian witness by States which are still able to afford to allow differences of conviction within their boundaries. So it was with Gandhi in India. Various forms of absolutist testimony have been tolerated within social structures sufficiently stable and secure to afford such non-conformity.

No community can dispense with an element of coercion and enforced discipline among its members. The difference between violent and non-violent resistance is only one of degree. Neither form can be justified from the Sermon on the Mount; and the pacifist, if he is to be consistent, must consent to go all the way to anarchy, with all the confusion and suffering anarchy implies. The possibility of the use of force is necessary to maintain order and justice, and without order and justice freedom degenerates into licence, and chaos returns to reign.

But a Church which forced its pacifists outside its membership would do harm to itself as well as to them. They may be no heretics, but have a special vocation to give their testimony to this aspect of truth as they see it. The typical Christian attitude to overcome evil is not to fight it and master it, though we Christians may be forced into such resistance where there is no other way.

Even grace cannot dispense with law. The Church cannot live *in vacuo*. And no Church, however strong its own convictions and even its willingness for martyrdom, has any right to rob the State within which it exists of the weapons it requires to maintain justice, order, and liberty, so far as these are ever attained in any State. Some time ago it used to be urged that what was needed was a people pledged to non-resistance to give the world an example, even at the cost of martyrdom. We have now had several such examples. We are confronted with the martyrdom of many peoples. We have seen how cunningly the unwillingness of certain nations to go to war has been exploited, how the strength of pacifism has weakened their power to stand by others at the risk of war.

On the other hand we see a very real danger if the Church unhesitatingly casts in its lot with the State, consecrates a war as not only a just war (which a State may well wage, as its aim is justice), but as a holy war (if there can be any such thing), and throws all its weight into the scales as a useful moral weapon of the military arm. We had some experience of that in 1914–18, and we are still suffering from the effects of it.

Even at the risk of seeming to speak with two voices, it is good and right for the Church, while affirming its own loyalty and support to the State in waging what we may believe to be a just war, to protect the pacifist testimony as a witness to those absolutes usually referred to as the Sermon on the Mount. No political unit can take these as the items of its policy, no business can make anything of it on a policy of the other cheek and the second mile, no institution of any kind, the Church included, can proceed as if these were the articles of its association. But all of us, our individual conduct and our corporate activities, are judged by this "impossible" ideal which yet remains "supremely relevant" and regulative for us and all our doings. The only one who could live in this way was the Saviour. That was His vocation and His achievement as the Lord of all life. Our vocation as His disciples is to follow Him as closely as we can, and to translate into all the realities and necessities and relativities of our daily lives as much as we can of His Spirit that moved Him and led Him to the Cross and raised Him from the dead. We are not called to become the saviours of society, but to be the disciples of the Saviour and witnesses to His resurrection. There is room and need for the pacifist testimony to the absolute ethic in this regard; there may be need for some to adopt a life of celibacy and poverty as they are "called" to follow Christ. All such testimonies are, or at least may be, facets of the truth, as that was revealed by Jesus, in which we may see something of the radiance as the glory of God shines from the face of Jesus Christ. None of us has a monopoly of truth—that should keep us humble: none is deprived of all share of that light that lighteth every man that cometh into the world. It is no longer true that intense belief must show itself in fanatical and pharisaic persecution. There is a difference between truth and testimony, but it is our stern duty to bear testimony to the truth as the truth has been revealed to us, tempering our convictions with the charity due towards others, who with equal sincerity have different perspectives, both of truth and of duty. That is inevitable on the doctrine of vocation. The non-pacifist lion and the pacifist lamb may lie down together in one Church with tolerable amity and mutual respect. We are "members" one of another. We need one another in our fellowship. We act as complementary organs of one body, and help one another to see more of truth and duty than any of us would see by himself.

If this issue had arisen in the Church, say, a hundred years ago, it would almost certainly have caused the secession of certain groups on a sectarian basis. The essence of the sectarian spirit is the erection of some particular principle into an absolute of universal validity and obligation, so that those who hold it can no longer recognize its relativity in regard to other principles, and its special application only to certain individuals or groups or situations. Rome provides for such heroic absolutism not only in its monastic system, but in the institution of "Orders". Protestantism till lately had little provision for those with a special vocation to bear testimony to some particular truth or value. Generally speaking, Church officials and courts tended to inquire if the proposal in question was for everybody, and if it were not, to withhold approval. Now, on a vocational ethic, we recognize the value of certain proposals consists precisely in the fact that they are *not* for everybody, but cannot be condemned as heresies accordingly, nor can a Church which refuses to identify itself with them be liable to a charge of apostasy. The treatment of pacifists by Church and State in the last two wars is an interesting illustration of the advance made towards a vocational ethic in which conviction and charity can each enlighten the other. But, on the other hand, if we think this attitude marks real moral progress, we must remember that the State could be tolerant and considerate only so long as those who hold these conscientious convictions were so small a proportion that their non-conformity did not seriously impede the war effort, or embarrass the State by withdrawing from it the moral support of a large proportion of its citizens. A nation at war finds it difficult to concede freedom to preach as well as to practise pacifism. But in the Church we have learnt to respect the integrity of those who feel a special vocation to bear witness to this "absolute" as an authentic reading of certain features of the Gospel, though the Church as a whole, recognizing its social responsibilities, over against the State, cannot identify itself with such testimony with sectarian absolutism.

To the outsider this difference of attitude seems to be merely "speaking with two voices" in a bewildering way. The Roman Church solves the problem by providing for and defining the limits of such special vocations. It takes a great deal of humility and patience for Protestants to try to explain the difference between truth and testimony, and give the reasons for the apparently contradictory voices.

Even though the Protestant Churches may not have been successful in explaining this to the man in the street, it is surely a hopeful sign that the pacifist element in the Churches no longer attempts to challenge the Church to identify itself with absolute pacifism, nor do the Churches brand their pacifists as heretics or traitors. We acquiesce in difference, without condoning indifferentism. But it is increasingly difficult to justify this distinction, especially when the modern State insists on all its citizens making their utmost possible contribution to a war effort, even in a "cold war". The Church must in war and peace stand by the principle that conscience must not be coerced in the interests of military or economic efficiency. Administrative convenience must never be the last word. This is the fundamental principle behind *habeas corpus* and many other enactments which even war-time exigencies could only partially suspend. If, as seems likely, we are to spend the next half-century on a semi-war footing, we must remain constantly vigilant to prevent the sacrifice of principles so vital to democracy on the altar of expediency. *Salus populi suprema lex* is simply not true if it interprets *salus* as mere *safety*, but it is true if it means *salvation*. The ruthlessness of the totalitarian regimes overrides the individual citizen's rights and privileges, and even liquidates himself if and when public expediency finds him inconvenient. We must beware, as we confront this ruthlessness, of the danger of conforming to the methods of the enemy and trying to beat him at his own game, at the cost of sinking to his level of brutality. War situations are never good schools of Christian virtues, and cold war continued indefinitely, and affecting the whole population of all nations, may become a moral blight. The Church in protecting its pacifists is contributing substantially to the respect for human personality and sincere, even if inconvenient, testimony, and therefore to the cause of true liberty, which is as near an absolute value as anything can be.

Chapter Six

AMBITION, DESTINY, AND VOCATION

THE current psychological jargon of our time has familiarized everybody with such words as "libido", "élan vital", and "the will to power". There is in us all, however we express it, an instinctive "urge" that seeks satisfaction and fulfilment. Freud says its primitive and typical form is sex, in his comprehensive sense of the word; others interpret it differently. Whatever it is, it is there, a thing to be reckoned with, to which are due the noblest achievements of mankind and also the craving for wealth and power that has corrupted the whole world around us. What are we to make of ambition, that "last infirmity of noble minds"? Is it a thing evil in itself, with no place in the religious life? Then what of the "ambition" of the great missionary pioneers like David Livingstone; of Churchmen like Thomas Chalmers, John Wesley, William Booth, and D. L. Moody; of Florence Nightingale; of statesmen like Cromwell, Gladstone and Abraham Lincoln, who scorned delights to live laborious days, and enriched the world by the fruits of their devoted lives? Sir Walter Moberly says "ambition is not a Christian virtue".[1] J. H. Oldham says: "Christianity, in fundamental contrast to Buddhism, recognizes that ambition is of the essence of religion."[2] Lord Charnwood says: "Ambition, commensurate with the powers

[1] *The Crisis in the University*, p. 273.
[2] *International Review of Missions*, Jan., 1921, p. 70.

which each man can discover in himself, should be frankly recognized as a part of Christian duty."[1]

Where are we to place Napoleon, Bismarck, and Cecil Rhodes? Both Hitler and Mussolini believed themselves to be the man of destiny for their respective countries, with a clear mission to lead their people to an empire. Spengler, in his *Decline of the West*, singles out Cecil Rhodes as "the first precursor of a Western type of Caesars, whose day is to come though still distant. He stands midway between Napoleon and the force-men of the next centuries."[2] He is one of the typical "men of the Renaissance."[3] "I see in Cecil Rhodes the first man of a new age. He stands for the political style of a far-ranging Western, Teutonic and especially German future, and his phrase 'expansion is everything' is the Napoleonic reassertion of the indwelling tendency of *every* Civilization that has fully ripened—Roman, Arab or Chinese. It is not a matter of choice—it is not the conscious will of individuals, or even that of whole classes or peoples that decides. The expansive tendency is a doom, something daemonic and immense, which grips, forces into service, and uses up the late mankind of the world-city stage, willy-nilly, aware or unaware. Life is the process of effecting possibilities, and for the brain-man there are *only extensive* possibilities."[4] We need not follow Spengler further in his assertion that "*the soul is the complement of its extension*", or accept his peculiar interpretation either of personality or of history. The whole story of Rhodes illustrates the theme of Greek tragedy, with power leading to *hubris* (pride), and, since the gods ruled the world and would not brook any human interference with their prerogatives, to *nemesis*. But the subject is not confined to Greek tragedy. It is the contemporary tragedy whose actors we all are. Nietzsche glimpsed some of its inner meaning. So did Kierkegaard. But the Titanism Spengler foretold, writing in 1914–18, appeared a century

[1] *Abraham Lincoln*, p. 160.   [2] *Op. cit.*, I, p. 37.   [3] *Op. cit.*, I, p. 349.
[4] *Op. cit.*, I, p. 37.

before he thought it would. We may differ as to whether we are witnessing and living through Spengler's *Decline of the West* or Demant's *Decline of Capitalism* as an economic system, which exalted economic above ethical values and so was "eccentric" to the true providential order of events. But we must not allow philosophical theorists to interpret and adapt our truly Christian values and virtues, except in so far as such values and virtues are relative to the times and must change with them.

Over against the "men of destiny" can we, with Nietzsche, represent Christianity as a "slave morality", with an illusory ideal "kingdom" inhabited by nit-wits? Are the meekness and humility of the truly Christian life characteristics of the poor-spiritedness of those who simply do not have the "guts" to rend from "nature red in tooth and claw" the power and opportunity their natural talents require and deserve?

"Blessed are the meek, for they shall inherit the earth" is not a glorification of nit-wits. Moses was the typically "meek" man of the Old Testament and Moses was no nit-wit or quietist. It was Moses who interceded for Israel, and said: "Oh, this people have sinned a great sin, and have made them gods of gold. Yet now, if thou wilt forgive their sin—; and if not, blot me, I pray thee, out of thy book which thou hast written" (Ex. 32: 31, 32). There spoke the true leader and priest of his people. St. Paul was no nit-wit example of slave morality. "For I could wish that myself were accursed from Christ for my brethren, my kinsmen according to the flesh." (Romans 9: 3) He had been taught by Christ to care so supremely for his fellow men that he was willing to be shut out from grace if that might win them salvation. Both self-renunciation and self-assertion can no further go in nobility, for the shadow of the Cross had fallen across his life. Nor does the Church through its long and chequered history, enriched by so many emphatic personalities, give much support to the belief current to-day that religion takes all the life out of a man. Rather it brings new and apparently superhuman possibilities into life, and incidentally makes human life both significant and secure.

What we have to realize is that our religion recognizes and provides for the fulfilment of those fundamental things in human nature. If Freud is right and sex (in Freud's sense of sex) is *the* fundamental thing in our make-up, then a religion whose central belief is that "God is love" (*agapé* not *eros*) becomes supremely relevant as the true and only satisfactory sublimation of that primitive urge. In any case a true sense of vocation is the only adequate sublimation of the primitive pugnacious urge which, if perverted, leads to all the extravagances and cruelties of "vaulting ambition". Properly understood, no one ever was so ambitious as Jesus, His ambition being to establish the Kingdom of God. St. Paul, St. Francis, Luther, Shaftesbury, Livingstone —for the driving force behind such men ambition is an altogether inadequate and poverty-stricken word. These men never asserted themselves in a selfish sense, but gave and claimed everything for their cause and their Master. And they had so true an appreciation of the close relationship between means and ends that they never attempted to gain spiritual ends by material means that contradicted their aims. As an illustration, both Rhodes and Livingstone had dreams for Africa, and noble dreams they were. Both men had elements of nobility of character, and deep passionate loyalties. But by the standards either of purity of motive or of spiritual achievement there can be no possible comparison between them. The one takes his place as of right in the true succession of apostles, saints, and martyrs; while the other remains, for all his dreams, achievements and benefactions, empire-builder though he was, a man of the world, with all his actions stained with the earth of an unregenerate pagan character, magnificent but unredeemed. Livingstone was not wanting in faults of character, any more than was Florence Nightingale or St. Paul himself. But there was the quality of the Cross in them that the world fails to find in its rich men and conquerors.

In this connection we may recall the friendship and affinity that arose between Cecil Rhodes and General Gordon, and the respect and almost envy with which Rhodes seems to have regarded General Booth of the Salvation Army. Aristotle says that in true tragedy there must be a certain bigness in the characters, and this moral grandeur belongs to all these three men. Rhodes thought Gordon a fool for refusing a roomful of gold as reward for quelling the Taiping Rebellion, but when he heard of General Gordon's death in Khartoum, he seems to have regretted that he had not joined him in the Sudan. He himself rejected the opportunity to amass "roomfuls" of gold in order to nurse his dying friend Pickering. Avarice, as Spengler saw, was never Rhodes's motive, nor was it mere brute power, but power to accomplish the "big ideas" which required gold for their realization. The trouble with Rhodes was that he thought that as the man of destiny he could make his own code of morals, and to gain his ends he would stoop to the most unscrupulous means. The historian, the philosopher, and the theologian cannot severally or conjointly answer the questions whether, and if so why, Africa needed its Rhodes as well as its Livingstone. But when all is said and done, the story of Livingstone is a study in consecration, while the story of Rhodes is mainly one of achievement, with subsequent *hubris* and *nemesis*. Spengler is quite right that in history he will take his place among the great Romans, but Livingstone stands among the great saints. The difference is the difference between pride and humility, between selfishness and unselfishness, between a man who believes he is the centre of his universe, and a man who knows God is at the centre, and knowing this, worships Him. In short it is the difference between the converted and the unconverted. It was no mistake that led Paul to emphasize *pleonexia* (covetousness) as the root vice and most dangerous idolatry.

Every virtue has its corresponding vice. A sense of vocation gives a man inspiration, but all inspiration is not of God, and the devil finds apt instruments in persuading men of ability that they are also men of destiny. Mussolini was described as "the man sent by Providence" by the Pope when he gave him his blessing. A true sense of vocation so enhances a man's normal powers that he can escape from the limitations of what is apparently humanly possible. Even a perverted sense of vocation can for a season promote such exalted powers. How is it that those portents of our time, Hitler, Stalin and Mussolini, and if one may mention him in the same breath, Winston Churchill, are apparently delivered from the doubts and hesitations and self-questionings that beset the rest of men, except that somehow they have come to think of themselves as the agents of some higher power, either God or their nation elevated into a kind of racial deity. Hitler said: "I am Germany", and claimed divine authority for his policy, as Napoleon said "policy is destiny". He was the only god there was for himself and for millions of his fellow-countrymen. That was the Promethean tragedy of Germany and Europe. Rhodes, a minister's son, began to become obsessed with the same infatuation of omnipotence, and his clay feet in the end proved unable to bear the weight of such an idol. "Power tends to corrupt," says Lord Acton, "and absolute power corrupts absolutely. Great men are almost always bad men. . . ."[1] "Big ideas are essential to progress," as Rhodes said. So are big men, but humility in greatness is quite as important as the truth of the big ideas. Titanism is not enough. Not only so, it brings its own destruction.

Two things distinguish the sense of vocation of the man of God from the self-seeking of the ambitious careerist. First, the former accepts his tasks from God upon his knees with a deep and humble and penitent sense of responsibility towards another whose servant he is, in an attitude of wor-

[1] *Historical Essays and Studies*, p. 504.

87

ship which, if sincere, is an almost perfect antiseptic to arrogance and selfishness. There are, of course, disconcerting instances where men made in a big mould have dominated their fellows, and at the same time have believed and practised a kind of religion that seems to have made them more ruthless, because they believed they were the instruments of God. Bismarck, even after a day spent in what seems to us almost diabolical Realpolitik, read his chapter from the Bible, said his prayers, and slept like a child. But Bismarck was no moral monster.

It is not enough that ambition should stop short of "defiance of the providential order";[1] that a Frederick and a Bismarck may be restrained from the *hubris* of a Napoleon. "Instead of becoming Napoleons they provided perhaps the two most remarkable examples in modern history of men who called a halt to a career of conquest, precisely because they had a curious awareness of the importance of the moral element in history."[2] A true sense of vocation is not merely a restraining influence to set bounds to the lust for power, it has power to transform that lust into devotion and to keep that devotion free from fanaticism.

Vocation cannot be understood in its fullest sense except in its relation to forgiveness and justification.[3] So understood, it becomes the inevitable issue of conversion,[4] the subjective correlate and response to Providence[5] and the governing principle of Christian behaviour. "*The solution of the outstanding problems of ethics is to be sought in terms neither of utilitarianism, however ideal, nor of Intuitionism, but of Vocation* . . . as the chief practical problem of ethics is solved,

---

[1] Butterfield, *Christianity and History*, p. 103.
[2] *Ibid.*, p. 49.
[3] See Ritschl, *Justification and Reconciliation*, pp. 434-72, and Brunner, *Divine Imperative*, pp. 198-207.
[4] See Isaiah 6; Acts 9: 15 and 13: 2; and Galatians 1; 11-24.
[5] "The idea of the Calling and of the Call is unintelligible apart from that of Divine Providence." Brunner, *The Divine Imperative*, p. 200. "It is evident that the whole doctrine of Providence is involved." W. Temple, *Nature, Man and God*, p. 407.

not by volition, but by conversion, so the chief theoretical problems are solved not by reference to a Categorical Imperative, but by reference to Vocation."[1] There can be no doubt of the sincerity of Cromwell's religion, nor of the reality of his "mission", but he was not exactly pussy-footed in Ireland. And we have the example of many Old Testament characters who sometimes did very queer things "in the name of the Lord". But if we want to see the connection between conversion and mission at its best we have the classical instances (already referred to) of Isaiah and St. Paul (Acts, chapter 9).[2]

Even a drastic and thorough conversion sometimes only succeeds in transferring a previous ambition to a different object. Perhaps the best recent study of this is in Lockhart's *Life of Cosmo Gordon Lang*: "I paid little attention to the service and less to the sermon, preached, I don't know about what, by the curate. But I had a strong sense that something was about to happen. I was not in the least excited; there was no sort of nervous tension; I had only prayed in a rather weary way during the service in some such manner as this— 'I can't go on with this strange struggle. End it, O God, one way or another. If there *is* anything real, anything of Thy will, in this question, help me to answer it.' Then suddenly, while the unheeded sermon went on, I was gripped by a clear conviction. It had all the strength of a masterful inward voice. 'You are wanted. You are called. You must obey.' I knew at once that the thing was settled. The burden of the long struggle dropped. My mind was free . . . a wave of such peace and indeed joy as I had never known before filled my whole being. . . . All my prayers had the one refrain: 'I obey and I am free!' Later the words came to my mind: 'I will run the way of Thy commandments when Thou hast set my heart at liberty.' . . . If there be a personal God, if He is ever concerned with or speaks to the individual spirit, He then

---

[1] William Temple, *op. cit.*, p. 407.
[2] See A. B. Davidson, *The Called of God, passim*.

and thus spoke to me. I have staked my life on this. . . . I dare not doubt its truth."[1]

When he left the Church he was already a candidate for Holy Orders. From childhood he had dreamed of becoming Prime Minister, or Lord Chancellor, now his ambition was to be Archbishop of Canterbury, and within two years of his ordination as priest he playfully signed himself "C. G. Cantuar". The whole subsequent story is an admirable illustration of an imperfectly sublimated sense of ambition. This is probably the reason why the book ends in sadness. The same may be said of an even more revealing autobiography, Lord Reith's *Into the Wind*.[2]

It is hard for us to imagine in heaven Oliver Cromwell in the same "mansion" with St. Francis of Assisi, but diverse though the types of character required by the world and contained within the Church we can imagine these two getting on well, but not either or both settling down comfortably beside Napoleon, still less Adolf Hitler. Ambition often masquerades in the guise of vocation, indeed it often borrows many of the noblest features of a true sense of vocation, just as a sense of vocation often degenerates into mere ambition, or becomes tainted with elements of arrogance. Ecclesiastical history has not yet seen the last conflict between prophet and priest; but if the essence of true religion be as the prophet Micah (6: 8) said: "What doth the Lord require of thee, but to do justly, and to love mercy, and to walk humbly with thy God"—then in the end no man is fit either to teach or to command his fellows unless he has first learned his own true attitude of penitence and humility before God.

The second real difference between vocation and ambition is in the use a man makes of his fellows. The truly religious man will remember that they are never to become mere

[1] Lockhart, *op. cit.*, pp. 64-65.
[2] Compare with this the remarkable story of the conversion in successive stages of "Rabbi" Duncan in the Biographical Introduction to A. B. Davidson's *The Called of God*, especially pp. 30-32.

pawns in the game, kulaks to be liquidated, Jews to be persecuted, Poles to be deported, labour to be exploited, cannon fodder to be conscripted and thrown into the battle, without any regard to their rights as human beings, in philosophical language "ends in themselves, never mere means to the ends of others". When Jesus links together in the summary of the whole duty of man God and our neighbour, He makes it quite clear that for His disciples there must be respect for the personality of every man, made in the image of God, redeemed at the cost of the blood of Jesus Christ. When ambition seizes a man or when he disguises his ambition under the pretext of a divine mission, the true nature of his motives and ends will reveal themselves in the callousness of his methods and his lack of sensitiveness to the needs and claims of others. It is this that distinguishes Livingstone from Rhodes and in general the man with a real mission from the egoist careerist and adventurer, even though the latter may honestly believe himself to be the man of destiny. Perhaps the ego-Catholic is the most dangerous perversion of vocation that disturbs all denominations.

What is true of individuals is true also with some qualification of nations and groups. The classical though not the only case of a nation which believed it had a mission from God is, of course, as we have seen, the Jews. *It is indeed a sense of vocation which makes a nation.* The Jews have survived incredible hardships, persecutions, and temptations, because they still believe ardently in the divine mission of their people. Nothing else could have held them together and given them such amazing spiritual pertinacity. And where such a sense of vocation is lacking in the spiritual life of a nation it becomes enervated and decadent, with a subtle demoralization that neither education nor legislation can either check or reverse. Something of the sort, "a loss of nerve", a lack of direction and purpose, and general aimlessness, seems to have been behind the decay of both the Greek and the Roman Empires, and behind the decline and fall of many other empires as well. "Where there is no vision the people perish" (Proverbs 29: 18). On the other hand, the contrast between pre-Hitler and post-Hitler Germany, and pre-fascist and post-fascist Italy showed us the enormous access of power that comes to a nation when they are aroused from apathy to believe that they count for something in the world. This power may be a mere galvanic shock producing a semblance of real spiritual life. We may like it or we may not, we may deplore the revival of cruelty that recalls the worst brutalities of the world's darkest ages, but we must not, and indeed we cannot, deny that something radical and in some sense irrevocable happened in both these lands, and is happening in Russia and elsewhere under the influence of Communism. Something new and very terrible has been born in the world, something that might have been divine but has become demonic. Compared with the fierce and ruthless powers let loose in the world, the power of religion, as we believe and practise our religion, looks trivial and pathetic. And yet the only hope that the world may be able to emerge from this age of crisis and conflict is that there should flame up in the Church this sense of vocation from God, making men sure-footed in the midst of bewilderment, hopeful in despair, and providing leaders in all walks of life who seek something higher than and different in kind from their own selfish ambitions. "In the missionary idea the will to power finds its deepest satisfaction and human nature seems to rise to its greatest height."[1] In a word, we can only counter the demonic claims of a perverted and ruthless sense of vocation, spreading wreckage and misery and misleading multitudes, by a revival of the real thing in individuals, in the Church and in the nation, giving men something to live for, and to live by.

The world as a whole is weary of imperialism. This may be in the case of the great powers a revulsion from power-politics or merely the satiety of the boa-constrictor, sleeping

[1] J. H. Oldham, I.R.M., 1921, p. 71.

till his victim is digested. It is easy to be cynical about imperialism, almost as easy as to be cynical about capitalism. This reaction from imperialism may betoken decadence, the softening of the moral stamina that in the Roman Empire began at the outposts because the heart of the empire was no longer sound. There is in our new impoverishment since the last war less truth in the jibe that like a converted burglar we view with real alarm the depredations of others, while we live more or less comfortably off on our own ill-gotten gains. "We can now afford a conscience." But there is surely more in it than that. We are developing a sensitive conscience about our dealings with other nations, within and outside the empire, that cannot be explained cynically on the grounds that we can *now* afford a conscience, or that we have been compelled to treat more deferentially peoples in Africa and Asia who are no longer willing to believe themselves in any sense inferior to ourselves.

The tragedy is that this slackening of political imperialism has resulted in a loss of sense of purpose and "mission" in Church and State. Not by mere accident the period of industrial and imperialist expansion coincided with the great missionary developments of last century. And now, when political imperialism is flagging, and in all lands are being raised banners with many strange devices, the climate is becoming more and more inhospitable to the Gospel, and the Church is becoming less sure of its missionary vocation. Is it because Christendom seems to be crumbling under our feet? Or because missionaries no longer go as representatives of a superior culture? Or are we now experiencing in Church and State that same "loss of nerve" that in so many other cases has marked the fall of an empire and the end of an era? Only the future will show. If we have lost our absolutes, nothing can redeem individuals from loneliness and insecurity, not even the mass-hysteria of the new collectivisms. Nothing can save our social structures from totalitianism except a revival of a true religious sense of vocation, creating the freedom and order of a responsible society, which traces its rights and duties, and indeed all social authority and individual significance and purpose to their source in the sovereign will of God.

Chapter Seven

VOCATION AS THE CLUE TO ECCLESIASTICAL DIVERSITY—
VOCATION IN THE CHURCH

ONE of the signs of the times is the revival of apocalypticism. There is everywhere a strong reaction from what
one might call evolutionism in religious thinking, with its
tendency to a comprehensive and tolerant and flabby humanism. The spiritual climate of Europe has changed in a most
marked way in the last few years.

The world situation confronting Christianity is more
threatening than anything in history since the early days of
Islam. Is a merciless Marxism to win the East? Are Russia
and the countries east of the Iron Curtain going to become
lost provinces of Christianity as were the countries of North
Africa when they were overwhelmed by Islam?

Everywhere the old order is changing. In politics liberalism is in full retreat, with its ideals of freedom and orderly
progress. Ever since Marx we have been forced, however un-
willingly, to admit the close correspondence that exists between our ecclesiastical, our political, and our economic
the doctrine of *laissez-faire* in economics, and the emergence
institutions. With the collapse of liberal ideas in politics, of
of a planned economy everywhere, we must be prepared for
profound changes in our ecclesiastical institutions, if they
are not merely to survive, but to influence the world of our
day creatively and redemptively.

For instance, the heyday of liberalism in Great Britain

corresponded with the great period of Free Trade and *laissez-faire*. Along with these went the policy of Voluntaryism so prominent especially in Nonconformist Churches, and the Disestablishment movement, which has had strong supporters even within the Church of England since the rejection of the Deposited Prayer-Book. These three, political liberalism, economic *laissez-faire*, and ecclesiastical voluntaryism, were closely allied to one another; in fact they were simply different versions of the one attitude to public life. Now the whole climate has changed. It is not so much that our questions have been answered and our problems solved, but we no longer ask the same questions, and we are confronting new and more dangerous problems. We are face to face with the Corporative State. Even in the countries which have not as yet adopted this type of organization it is recognized that the old era of haphazard opportunism in politics and economics is at an end, and men are hastily attempting to set their house in order by formulating plans of political control, where formerly everything was left to the unregulated operation of the supposed laws of supply and demand. Control is the order of the day, and inevitably so if we are to be saved from chaos, with violent fluctuations of markets and prices, appalling unemployment, and the inevitable nemesis of war. But man is more than plan, and in the welfare state, as in every state, we require clear thinking and deep convictions on the human values that should determine the form of our social structures.

The Corporative State, erected on a purely secular basis, working for purely secular ends by methods which know no law except their effectiveness, is rapidly coming to be recognized for what it is, *the negation of God erected into a system*.

On the other hand, as a rival totalitarianism, stands the Roman Church, which found much in common with fascist totalitarianism, and indeed was more at home with such an authoritarian régime than it ever has been with the industrialized capital-labour democratic set-up. Now it has declared war against communist totalitarianism, for obvious reasons, as communism has developed into a pseudo-religion. But Rome has challenged Moscow directly on the political level, so that we see the Vatican and the Kremlin confronting one another as rival absolute and incompatible political powers. Protestantism, as represented at Amsterdam, has avoided open collision on the political plane, partly because Protestantism does not claim political authority as does Rome, partly because Protestantism is not complacent about the spiritual sufficiency of the present capital-labour set-up and is afraid of allying itself with the forces of economic and political reaction against all change. It looks sometimes as if Protestantism were to be crushed between the upper and the nether millstones, of ruthless Roman Catholicism and equally ruthless Communism. On the other hand, some predict that in the new atmosphere of tension, political, economic and military, which is apparently going to be the climate of the world for many years to come, only three forms of belief are strong enough to survive—Roman Catholicism, Calvinism, and Communism. For, it is maintained, in a world where the soul has been deprived of its normal sources of security, and all or almost all accepted patterns of conduct have been disturbed, only these three can provide the necessary absolutes in which men can find safety and fellowship and peace.

We have yet to see how religion can survive and function under a communist state, where the official doctrine is that religion is psychologically an escape-mechanism, and politically a means of consecrating exploitation and maintaining the *status quo*. We have also still to see what ecclesiastical changes will be required in the set-up of institutional religion in the welfare state.

Over against totalitarianism in Church and in State we Protestants maintain that our loyalty to any institution can only be conditional and never absolute. There are many who see the Church as the only possible or the best possible weapon with which to combat Communism. They are right in so far as they see that a spiritual movement like Communism cannot be challenged, contained and defeated by military strength, or military strength allied to economic resources. Communism offers a means of integration to men whose souls and social structures are obviously disintegrating, who have lost their absolutes and hence are lonely and afraid with the sinking feeling of insecurity in the end of an era.[1] It is no use offering men freedom when freedom means exploitation or unemployment in time of peace and anonymous destruction in time of war. Men no longer desire such freedom, they are afraid of it. The ballot-box means nothing to men whose lives are purposeless, whose work contains no joy, and who are drifting like ships that have lost their moorings and have their steering broken down.

We have seen fanatical galvanized heroism in Fascism, we see it also in Communism. But we must not allow the Church to be manipulated into a bulwark of social reaction. To us Protestants the aims and methods of the corporative state are anathema, because they deny the freedom of the individual conscience and the rights of the individual soul. It is quite true that a free Church can exist and function properly only within a free State. It is no less true, though not so often recognized, that a free State is impossible without the spiritual support and nourishment of a free Church. *The countries which have most successfully achieved political freedom have been the countries where there has been greatest ecclesiastical diversity.* Figgis goes so far as to say that "political liberty is the residuary legatee of ecclesiastical animosities".[2] If for animosities he would write diversities we could not quarrel with him. In all our thought about Christian unity we must remember how much our social heritage has been enriched by our diversities. In Scotland one of the things prominently before us in framing the recent union of the Churches was

[1] See Erich Fromm, *The Fear of Freedom, passim.*
[2] *From Gerson to Grotius*, p. 118.

the undoubted fact that in the past spiritual revival has almost always issued in secession or disruption. The Church of Rome in this has usually shown great ecclesiastical wisdom, though not always. It recognizes this universal spiritual tendency. Every breath of the Spirit seeks to clothe itself in an appropriate body, and Rome has learnt to provide for these new movements and to profit by them. It creates a new Order *within* the Church, with its own leaders, its spiritual Rule, and special functions. So the Church is enriched by these new movements, and they are enabled to bear testimony to the new light without being forced to seek relief of conscience in secession. Outsiders are seldom aware of the extraordinary complexity and even divergence of tendency within the Roman Church.

The Church of England also is learning this lesson of history. It now contains elements so heterogeneous that others wonder how it can maintain even the semblance of unity, still less the reality of spiritual fellowship, and the most rudimentary ecclesiastical discipline. But if the Anglican Church had always been as Catholic and comprehensive, it might quite possibly have brought or kept within its borders George Fox, the Wesleys, and William Booth, to say nothing of others.

In Scotland, with the vast majority of the population now within one Church, we are facing the same problem and learning the same lesson, and hoping and preparing, so that when the breath of the Spirit does come in revival, it will not mean, as it has almost always meant in the past, a secession or a disruption because the old ecclesiastical bottles cannot contain the new wine. We have now within the united Church of Scotland our extreme High Church party, our hot Evangelicals, our Modernists, our Fundamentalists, our Voluntaries and our Establishment men, our Pacifists and our Sanctionists, our Barthians and our Humanists, all within one communion. We recognize that as there is a better thing than Romanism, so there is a better thing than sectarianism, and we are not in education, for instance, any longer impaled on the dilemma of secularism or sectarianism. There is a better thing. We must abandon the old reproach of "our unhappy divisions", and begin to acknowledge how much we owe to the rich diversity of our denominational contributions to the one Body of Christ.

It is no accident that the Church, in response to the reaction towards authoritarianism in politics, is taking refuge in apocalypticism. This is true to type, and in accordance with the genius of our faith. In times of persecution the Church abandons the outworks of humanism, where it has given hostages to the world and is insecure because of treachery within the walls, and takes refuge within the impregnable keep of apocalypticism. Karl Barth is a pure apocalyptic prophet: there is to be no compromise with the world, no contact with it—humanism, liberalism, culture, and civilization, these are all classed with secular things; and to them all the Church, built on the Word of God, responds with a challenge and a stark negation. It is a sign of the times. When persecution breaks out the Church entrenches itself in apocalyptic, as for instance in the *Book of Revelation*, and waits like Wellington within the lines of Torres Vedras for the assaults of the enemy to exhaust themselves, before sallying forth again in missionary endeavour and programmes of social reform to convert souls and bring nearer the Kingdom of God.

In ethics as well as in theology the new note is becoming more distinctive. Reinhold Niebuhr is now described as "neo-orthodox", in spite of his radicalism, because of his reaction from theological liberalism.

This most interesting movement away from liberalism and towards apocalypticism has important and immediate ecclesiastical repercussions. Apocalyptic religion has its merits, but tolerance is not one of them, just as ascetic and evangelical religion is always apt to be intolerant and fanatical. That, of course, points to the necessity of cross-fertilizing each type of religious experience with the others in the fellowship of the Church. The Catholic needs to live in constant contact with the Sectary and the Mystic, if he is to be saved from formalism and barren ecclesiasticism. The Mystic becomes self-centred and apathetic, unless he is continually aroused by the Evangelist. The Evangelist is in grave moral danger, unless he is in a pastoral fellowship with the Christian community as well as in redeeming contact with individuals. Troeltsch has traced these threefold strands of Christian testimony throughout the history of the Church in his monumental *Social Teaching of the Churches*. There is also the parallel conflict between Temple and Synagogue, which itself is the lineal descendant of the Old Testament tension between priest and prophet. Whether we use the paradox, the polarity, the dialectical, or the dimensional phraseology to describe these tendencies, is of no very great importance. The main point is that we can see here as before how the principle of vocation enables us to unite deep conviction with broad charity. Authentic testimony can never be ultimate truth: the white light of truth is made up of the colours of the prism. No one can claim for himself or his denomination infallibility or exclusive possession of absolute truth, though each and all, if they be sincere and humble in their faith, can see and know enough for daily pilgrimage. That is one of the things that make an ordinary congregation of the Church of Christ so enormously interesting from the psychological point of view. It should be as far as possible a fellowship of all the varieties of religious experience. And the extent to which it can contain and benefit from their diversity is a proof of its possession of the Spirit of God, and of its successful proclamation of the Gospel of the grace and kingdom of God. The same is or ought to be true of our denominations, so far as these are justifiable as furthering the kingdom, each contributing its distinctive testimony according to its vocation.

There are some who look upon our denominational system as an unmitigated misfortune, an expression of the sin of schism which does anything but command the Gospel and promote the kingdom of God. "A denomination is that which ought not to exist." (Visser t'Hooft) Without attempting to defend all aspects and aberrations of denominationalism, we should entertain the possibility that such a system in some form may be part of the purpose of God for the Church, and may become the best means of promoting the Kingdom. In hearing and reading some dissertations on Christian unity (which is frequently confused with Church union, a very different thing), one is sometimes tempted to believe that it is an offence against public decency for a man to have two ears, two eyes, two hands, two feet, ten fingers and ten toes!

It is a matter for congratulation that we have at last escaped from the endless relativity of humanistic ethics. But we have not yet, either in theology or in ethics, come to terms with the category of evolution, which is still the dominant conception in the biological world, and which looked at the first blush as if it were going to explain or explain away all our moral distinctions and values.[1] There is no doubt that the scientific procedure of describing everything in terms of the lowest category applicable has resulted in a general tendency to reduce all the values of our human life to their lowest terms. The worst instance of this is probably behaviourism in psychology. The result has been a widespread belief that there are no absolutes; beauty, truth, and goodness, are all merely relative terms, and man is the measure of all things. Pascal's reed which thinks has become the rod to determine all values, and unfortunately it has proved little better than a broken reed. That explains the disillusionment and pessimism of the humanists. A witty observer has described the prevailing temper of our day as one of "Stoicism in plus fours". Hence has come the flight from humanism, the "return to religion", which in too many cases means only an attempt to enlist religion on behalf of a faint-

[1] See John Baillie, *The Belief in Progress*, especially pp. 132-54.

ing humanist cause, or taking refuge in what T. S. Eliot calls a "catholicism of despair". Men thrust forward their hands towards anyone who seems to possess authority, and beseech him to put handcuffs on them to keep them from trembling. The return to authority in religion is partly a symptom of the similar trend in politics, economics, and culture generally, and partly a reaction from it in the case of those who are terrified by the new Moloch. The corporative state is at once the apotheosis and the nemesis of tendencies which have been growing upon European civilization since the Renaissance. The humanists, gazing in terror upon this awful apparition which claims to be their child, but in which they see only a reversion to barbarism, throw themselves under the protection of whatsoever gods there be.

In reaction from the evolutionary views to which everything was only a little more or less, a little better or worse, and denominational differences were at best a necessary evil, which became less and less of an evil as they became less necessary, it looks as if we may be approaching a period of intolerant and fanatical dogmatism in religion, in which it is going to be very difficult to conserve the real humanist values in our faith, and to temper conviction with charity. It is significant to observe how the new movements of our time, such as Barthianism and the Oxford Group, are becoming intensely fanatical and pharisaic.

It is the recognition of the real and inevitable relativity of our moral perspectives that leads many to scepticism, in despair of reaching any absolute values, and leads many more to trifle with such real and all-important distinctions as right and wrong, good and evil. Hence arises the moral indifferentism so common to-day, masquerading as toleration. "It all comes to the same thing in the end." "Evil is good a little less fully developed." Philosophical or secular ethics is unable to extricate itself from the toils of evolutionism and arrive at any absolute values. Even personality itself on humanistic terms is not an absolute value: it only becomes so with the advent of the Christian doctrine of the immortality of the soul in fellowship with God, which thus, strangely enough, becomes a political principle of the utmost value, and the only conclusive argument against the liquidation policy pursued against inconvenient individuals by the corporative state.

It is here that the principle of Vocation becomes so important for our times.

To us Christians our duty is relative, but not endlessly relative: it is relative to our vocation. Vocation is at once a principle of individuation and of integration, a justification of diversity and a means of promoting unity. Whereas the moral philosopher can only speak of "my station and its duties", as things arbitrarily determined for him, the Christian has in his hands a principle which serves to explain how duty can be absolute without being universal, how I may be sure this line of conduct is right for me, without necessarily proceeding at once to impose it without modification upon my neighbours as absolute and universally binding on them too. In short, this principle enables us to achieve one of the rarest things in the spiritual life—*a union of deep and passionate conviction with broad and tolerant and sympathetic charity for other people's convictions, opinions, and loyalties. What is the vocation of some need not necessarily be the duty of all.*

Since for us Christians both faith and conscience are but different aspects of one attitude to God and man, a variation in our conception of duty will invariably be accompanied by a corresponding variation in our beliefs. It is impossible to attain, and unwise to attempt to secure, absolute uniformity of belief unless and until there is identity of duty. That is to say, there will be variations of belief as and because there are perspectives of duty, and both relative to our vocation. So we arrive at *the root and the rationale of our religious diversities. They are not necessarily due to the moral perversity of the people who differ from us, but may indicate the part they are each expected to play in life to the glory of God.*

If we turn to Ephesians 4 we find, as one might expect, that this mention of vocation is closely linked to the distinctively Pauline teaching on the Body of Christ. Ephesians 4: 1–13, is quite conclusive on this important conjunction. It applies directly to the relations of individuals to one another and to the Church. The Church is meant to be a "cosmos of callings", where each of us finds the place God means us to fill and serves Him faithfully in it, remembering he is only a member of the One Body. We have seen how this Christian doctrine of vocation, as applied here to the Church and in 1 Corinthians 7 to the "secular" callings, supplies us with the Christian sublimation of ambition. A sense of vocation is the true and only sublimation of ambition. As opposed to the spirit that would discover and ruthlessly carve out a coveted position for itself, is the spirit that waits on bended knee for the guidance of God, then faithfully performs it. As against the other spirit, too common in our robotical age, that destiny is determined for or rather against us by fate or chance or accident, is this doctrine of vocation which means the purpose of grace which a personal God has for us as persons, living in fellowship in the community of faith.

But vocation is a principle of social integration as well as of social articulation. The Kingdom of God is also meant to be a "cosmos of callings", where each finds the place and work best fitted to his capacities, and serves God in it "with a perfect heart".

The ecclesiastical diversity which has been a feature of Christianity since its earliest days is an indication that there must always be differences of gifts and of vocation within the Body of Christ. Just as the variations in conscience from individual to individual are no proof that conscience is unreliable, but on the contrary show how concrete and practical conscience actually is, so the diversity of our attitudes in belief and procedure points to the varying contributions we are meant to bring to the Kingdom of God. Now we see through a glass darkly, we only know bit by bit. None of us has a monopoly of truth. God is not a Presbyterian, nor was Jesus even a European. The old Wesleyan lay-preacher quaintly read in Revelation 21 "and the twelfth was a Methodist". Unconsciously we each think our own is the only possible language of Canaan, like the old Scots landlady, whose lodger lay at the point of death, and "the puir laddie hadna a word o' the Gaelic, and he wadna ken what they said to him on the ither side". We are all more or less like that, but few of us are humble and wise enough to recognize the difference between our principles and our prejudices.

This does not lay us under any obligation to encourage and justify the aberrations and demonic pretensions of sectarianism; but it should open our eyes to certain things inherent both in the Gospel and in human nature, which make ecclesiastical uniformity as obsolete an ideal as the Holy Roman Empire. Even granted that denominational convictions and loyalties for many of us have no justification except that of "irrational" tradition and custom, still no good thing can come out of attempts to assimilate or sweep away our distinctive denominational characteristics in favour of a featureless catholicity, which, aiming at being ecumenical, might succeed at best in becoming scarcely or merely Roman. It is in accordance with the lessons of history to maintain that the Church has usually been most serviceable to God and most faithful in its witness to truth and righteousness and freedom as a broken Body. It may be that there is a fundamental mystical reason and necessity in this, involved in the genius of our faith. The Church crucified is for this earth, because it is not of this earth: the Church glorified is for heaven, where the temptations which in this imperfect world always beset the exercise of power can no longer pervert it from its purity and its mission. It is possible so to glorify the Church as a dominating institution that it loses its power to redeem the world. Indeed, that is part of the abiding message of the Reformation.

The genius of Protestantism will always reveal itself in

ecclesiastical diversities. Are we to deplore these as wilful perversions of the mind and purpose of God, or are we to respect them as historical and spiritual realities, with much more than a sentimental value? The future of Protestantism, and with it of the world, depends on our decision. There is no merit in non-conformity as such, but the ideal for the Church of Christ is not uniformity but charity. The forces that challenge our faith are now so ruthless and implacable that all is lost unless we take the Reformation more instead of less seriously, and press further our Protestant interpretation of the Gospel and that doctrine of the Church which is bound up with it. And in our attitude to our ecclesiastical institutions we must beware of the mistake, too often made in the history of the Church, of building up the kind of rigid organization which the first breath of the Spirit in revival must scatter to the four winds of heaven, in the interests of the kingdom of grace. "*The watchword of genuine Churchmanship is never 'the Church', but always and only 'Jesus Christ'.*"

It has been said that the Protestant Churches of to-day are in danger of repeating the mistake which led the League of Nations to shipwreck in the period between the wars. The Covenant of the League had no conception of the dynamic possibilities of nationalism till Hitler revealed them. So the earlier ecumenical movement tended to treat everything distinctive as if it were *ipso facto* deplorable. The formal uniting of bodies with different traditions and tenets may or may not be a good thing in its ultimate spiritual results. It may be only "a superficial union of Churches under an official exterior, a union in which theological differences would be so belittled that its Christianity might become wholly bogus".[1] The distinctive beliefs, principles and testimony may no longer have any real validity in the changed circumstances of a new era, and now be mere prejudices and superstitions. A prejudice is often a principle which has outlived its relevance.

[1] T. S. Eliot, *The Idea of a Christian Society*, pp. 45-46.

If still alive and effective, such distinctive principles may operate within one unity to enrich the harmony and widen the horizons of the body concerned. But if the union be motivated merely or chiefly for reasons of institutional efficiency or because of economic pressure, the spiritual advantage to be gained may be problematical. Each ecclesiastical, as each political or economic body, tends to develop its own "genius" or ethos. Most of the denominations of Protestant Christendom are no longer merely national. Anglicanism has now an international significance far beyond the British Commonwealth. Presbyterianism has an extraordinary capacity for acclimatization. Yet in South India and elsewhere we have convincing proof that the denominational distinctions of the West have no ultimate validity and sometimes little attraction and less relevance for the East. In China it is extremely possible that the Church for a number of years must depend on a part-time ministry, unless or until the vocation of a pastor or a priest is recognized as a legitimate employment, qualifying for a place in the community, and entitling the holder to a ration card. The easiest line of attack on the Church by a communist State is to class all ministers as non-producers, and so attempt to freeze out religious practices and beliefs by economic discrimination. Manipulation of the currency—a device made use of in recent years by almost all governments—may seriously cripple the Church as an institution without having recourse to anything that can be characterized as open persecution.

The vocation of the Church is to bear witness to the truth as it is in Jesus, to proclaim the Gospel of the Kingdom of God. This vocation is a far more important and ultimately more difficult thing than "to close the ranks against communism", or "to save Western civilization". Religion has in the past not seldom been used as an instrument of exploitation, and in the process has itself inevitably become the victim of such misuse. It is wise that the Church leaders of Protestantism, while regarding with open eyes the spiritual dangers inherent in Communism, should refuse to be stampeded into a crusade against Communism as a political system. At the same time, the Church should make its own position plain, by candid criticism of the injustices that have led men to turn to Communism in hope and in despair, as well as by warning and encouragement in the midst of the perils of these dangerous days. The international affiliations of our present-day denominations are of the utmost value in enabling us to correct patriotic distortions of relative values and of means into absolute ends. It remains to translate ecumenical dreams into terms of denominational loyalties, for to most people duty must still be construed in terms of definite denominational tasks. What will emerge as the structural set-up of Protestantism in east or in west no man knows. The ecumeniarchs who are struggling to frame Christian policy and strategy on world-wide lines have read their Hildebrand and are well aware of the inevitable arrogance of all institutions, civil or ecclesiastical, with absolute claims and absolute powers. For the rest, the plain folk, it remains to recognize that each and all of us, even in our imperfect loyalties and inarticulate beliefs, are still contributors to the one Body and sharers in the one Spirit, according to our vocation and the Providence that inspires the history of the Church and directs and overrules also the secular affairs of men.

It is possible that in the Providence of God non-religious ruthless Communism will accomplish in the east what the direct impact of Christianity in its missionary endeavour has largely failed to do, and by destroying what remains of the old religions, open new doors of opportunity for a missionary Church. Cyrus the unbeliever is claimed as an instrument of God and had his vocation and place in the purpose of the God he did not know.[1]

---

[1] Isaiah 45: 1-4. Read in this connection, as a study of history in the light of the call of God, chapters 40 to 55. Chapter 41: 1-5 is also supposed to refer to Cyrus.

It is probable that we are even now in the midst of revolutionary changes which will transform our existing ecclesiastical structures so drastically that even the Reformation will cease to be an adequate analogy, though there can be no question of "going back on the Reformation", unless we turn our backs on spiritual liberty and the achievements of the last four hundred years. It is more likely that Protestantism will be called on to take the Reformation more seriously than it has ever done, and the New Testament more seriously still.

PART TWO

THE CALLING

MAINLY SOCIOLOGICAL

Chapter Eight

VOCATION AND WORK

"IT is my contention that we have to-day a culture which is mainly negative. . . . I do not think it can remain negative, because a negative culture has ceased to be efficient in a world where economic as well as spiritual forces are proving the efficiency of cultures which, even when pagan, are positive; and I believe that the choice before us is between the formation of a new Christian culture, and the acceptance of a pagan one."

In these words, T. S. Eliot[1] has correctly diagnosed the dilemma of our time. In the previous chapters we have tried to indicate the importance of the principle of vocation, the sense of the world being under the control of God, and the sense that each life has a purpose in such a world. Such a sense makes a nation into a nation and a man into a truly autonomous moral person, when in fellowship by faith with God. We have tried to trace its importance in typical cases and applied it to typical problems such as pacifism and ambition. As we pass to a discussion of the particular problem of vocation in relation to work we might pause and ponder T. S. Eliot's wise analysis, and apply it to our present predicament.

Communism is spreading like a prairie fire all over the world, because, in spite of all its glaring faults and inadequacies and wickednesses, it represents a positive culture, a

[1] *The Idea of a Christian Society,* p. 13.

unified world-view, a relevant creed and a missionary programme, and indeed it seems to many to be the inevitable
social set-up for an industrialized and mechanized world.
This ruthless pagan culture is not a possibility, it is a fact,
and is now bidding to become the dominant factor in contemporary history. T. S. Eliot foresaw the necessity that a
negative society would either decline or "reform itself into
a positive shape which is likely to be effectively secular".[1]

"The system of working primarily for profit and mone-
tary reward is in process of disintegration. The masses are
craving for a stable standard of living, but over and above
that, they want to feel that they are useful and important
members of the community, with a right to understand the
meaning of their work and of the society in which they live.
. . . It is not only work but also leisure that is subjected to
entirely different interpretations and valuations. The puritan
sense of guilt in connection with leisure and recreation is still
at war with the emerging hedonistic cult of vitality and health.
The idea of privacy and contemplation, and of their value, is
at war with that of mass enjoyment and mass ecstasy."[2]

European civilization, like other civilizations, seems to
have "lost its nerve", and the Churches very largely to have
lost their sense of mission. The Church exists, to paraphrase
Brunner's words, to evangelize the world as a fire exists for
burning. European civilization is far from being a synonym
for Christianity: the word Christendom has faded out of our
vocabulary; but European civilization is so inescapably built
on the foundation of the Christian religion that when it loses
that religion it cannot but disintegrate. And similarly with
the character built on the rock of religion. All the meaning
goes out of life when it loses its vision of God and therefore
loses the sense of purpose and mission in life. As nature
abhors a vacuum, Communism rushes in to fill the vacuum
of the negative culture that has survived its religion. The
"god-shaped blank" (Julian Huxley) in godless lives is

[1] *Op. cit.*, p. 25.   [2] Karl Mannheim, *Diagnosis of our Time*, pp. 13–14.

swept and garnished ready for the seven devils to possess. And demon-possession is the only word adequate to describe what happens when men worship idols instead of God. We no longer need to go to primitive peoples for illustrations of such demonic obsessions. Fascism and Communism and similar portents of Titanism are now facts of history and factors in forming the climate in which our souls must breathe or suffocate.

It is too much to claim that the principle of vocation will restore the lost confidence of European culture and begin a process of integration again into a new culture to counteract the decadence and defeatism that are only too apparent. Only a revival of real religion can do that. But the principle of vocation does show us how religion can give a sense of wholeness, purpose and power to lives otherwise lonely, insignificant and hopeless. It gives men a sense of belonging not merely to something that matters, but to Someone who cares, and who holds in His hands the lives of men and the destiny of nations. It gives meaning to history and rescues men from the mass of indiscriminate mechanisms. Instead of, and in and through, the insistent push and pull of ruthless circumstance and fate, there is a voice speaking a name and saying: "Come unto me . . .", "Go ye into all the world . . .". To call this "Personalism" is in no sense to belittle it, but to affirm that all machinery in Church and State, ecclesiastical, political, industrial, economic and what-not, must treat men as ends in themselves because made in the image of God, whose worth is measured only by the Cross of Christ in all its dimensions of tragic and triumphant love.

But if we are to build up some sort of order of positive Christian values, we require to see how this principle of vocation affects work, and the whole economic basis of our civilization. It is partly because we do not have any clear conception of the place work should have in the scheme of things that Communism, which has such a conception, seems everywhere able to infiltrate into our strongest positions. It claims to build a new culture and social structure on labour, all values are derived from the toil of the plain man, and Christianity is dismissed from the picture of the new world Communism envisages, because of its incurably "bourgeois" origins, associations and effects. To the Communist Christianity is a gentleman culture of an *élite*, which is based on, implies, and encourages the exploitation of labour by property possessors and fattens the few on the toil of the proletariat. If we are to have any answer to such accusations we must examine the whole bearing of our Christian faith upon work, and the meaning and purpose of work in human life and in the plans of God for man. All the argument is based on the belief that there is such a God as is revealed by Jesus, and that we are living in a world where Providence is still the supreme reality and Grace our greatest hope.

What is work? Many people do not know. Some people do not care. Why do men work? How should they work? What is the relation of work to other activities and interests of man? "I like work: it fascinates me. I can sit and look at it for hours. I love to keep it by me: the idea of getting rid of it nearly breaks my heart."[1]

Man is a working animal. Does he work to live, or does he live to work? "It is the duty of the Church to see to it that the work serves God, and that the worker serves the work."[2] "Production is on account of man, not man of production."[3] "The reason why the Churches are in so much difficulty about giving a lead in the economic sphere is because they are trying to fit a Christian standard of economics to a wholly false and pagan understanding of work."[4] Further: "Work is not primarily a thing one does to live, but the thing one lives to do."[5] All these sayings cannot be true. None of them contains the whole truth.

[1] Jerome K. Jerome, *Three Men in a Boat*, Chap. XV.
[2] Dorothy Sayers, *Creed or Chaos*, p. 62.
[3] St. Antonio of Florence, quoted in *Our Culture*, p. 75 (ed. Demant).
[4] Dorothy Sayers, *op. cit.*, p. 53.
[5] *Op. cit.*, p. 53.

Ever since Aristotle, the close relation of pleasure to activity has been recognized. Ethics is still struggling with the problem of the respective relationships and values of duty and enjoyment. If we accept the view that work is the chief end of man, we not only find difficulty in ascribing proper values to leisure, but we cannot get a proper relationship between work and worship.

Another fascinating problem is the relation of work to art. The poet in the old Scots tongue was the *Makar* and indeed the word "poet" means "maker". One of the spiritual demands we make of work is that if it is to satisfy it must express personality. But art is one supreme expression of personality. We must recognize that in most artistic production terrible toil is involved, but the toil is not the end, nor is the artistic product complete in itself without the toil which produced it. If a process of manufacture is obviously producing beauty out of some raw material, it will be in some sense soul-satisfying, but the process by which it is produced may not itself tend to the expression or development of personality.

Civilization does not simply happen. It is man's supreme construction.[1] In the last resort a man's work will be spiritually satisfying if it is obviously contributing to the building-up of civilization. That is to say, if work be socially creative, it will usually have a good effect upon the personality of the worker; if it be not so creative, it will fail to express and develop that personality. Is work then merely a means to an end? If so, what is the end? Firstly, making things? Secondly, providing subsistence? Or, thirdly, developing character? Obviously work must fulfil these subjective and objective ethical requirements if it is to be satisfying and wholesome. If work itself is to be truly ethical, it must contribute to building both character and civilization; that is why a man who has lost interest in his work or whose work has no real sig-

[1] "The man-made surrogate for the Kingdom of God", V. A. Demant in *The Listener*, June 29, 1950, p. 1104.

nificance for him will never be in a spiritually wholesome condition, no matter how much he may earn, and also why the experience of unemployment is so devastating and demoralizing. The man who can find no work loses his self-respect, with the sense that he no longer has a status in the community.

But what is the status of a worker in the community, and how is it measured? Does our present ethical standard of values in this or in any other country implicitly or explicitly exalt the life of leisure above the life of toil and confine all possibilities of culture to the former? It is possible that Thomas Carlyle has something to teach us in the magnificent passage of *Sartor Resartus*:

> Two men I honour, and no third. First, the toilworn Craftsman that with earth-made Implement laboriously conquers the Earth, and makes her man's. Venerable to me is the hard Hand; crooked, coarse; wherein notwithstanding lies a cunning virtue, indefeasibly royal, as of the Sceptre of this Planet. Venerable too is the rugged face, all weather-tanned, besoiled, with its rude intelligence; for it is the face of a Man living manlike. O, but the more venerable for thy rudeness, and even because we must pity as well as love thee! Hardly—entreated Brother! For us was thy back so bent, for us were thy straight fingers and limbs so deformed: thou wert our Conscript, on whom the lot fell, and fighting our battles wert so marred. For in thee too lay a god-created Form, but it was not to be unfolded; encrusted must it stand with the thick adhesions and defacements of labour: and thy body, like thy soul, was not to know freedom. Yet toil on, toil on: *thou* art in thy duty, be out of it who may; thou toilest for the altogether indispensable, for daily bread.
>
> A second man I honour, and still more highly: Him who is seen toiling for the spiritually indispensable; not daily bread, but the bread of Life. Is not he too in his duty; endeavouring towards inward Harmony; revealing this, by act or by word, through all his outward endeavours, be they high or low? Highest of all, when his outward and his inward endeavour are one: when we can name him Artist; not earthly Craftsman only, but inspired Thinker, who with heaven-made Implement conquers Heaven for us! If the poor and humble toil that we

may have Food, must not the high and glorious toil for him in return, that he have Light, have Guidance, Freedom, Immortality?— These two, in all their degrees, I honour: all else is chaff and dust, which let the wind blow whither it listeth.

Unspeakably touching is it, however, when I find both dignities united; and he that must toil outwardly for the lowest of man's wants, is also toiling inwardly for the highest. Sublimer in this world know I nothing than a Peasant Saint, could such now anywhere be met with. Such a one will take thee back to Nazareth itself; thou wilt see the splendour of Heaven spring forth from the humblest depths of Earth, like a light shining in great darkness.[1]

There is no parallel to this in pagan literature—it is a product of the Gospel. Further it is a product of the Gospel as mediated through Thomas Carlyle's Protestant and Presbyterian traditions and environment. But Carlyle comes near to making a gospel of work, and this exaggeration has its dangers, more easily seen in 1951.

It is no use theorizing about the economic system unless and until we get some idea of what work is and is meant to be; and we cannot understand what work is meant to be except by realizing what man is and is meant to be. It is a commonplace among all thinkers about religion that to understand the meaning and purpose of human life, we must get a true idea of God and of man's relation to Him. If that relation be one of worship, it will also be one of service, and we get the saying in one form attributed to St. Augustine: "*laborare est orare*". Here again Carlyle has a word for us. "Properly speaking, all true Work is Religion, and whatsoever Religion is not Work may go and dwell among the Brahmins. . . . With me it shall have no harbour. Admirable was that of the old monks, '*Laborare est Orare*, work is worship'."[2] We shall consider this more fully when we come to treat of the importance of the monastic system in working out the Christian idea of work and the rhythm between work and worship.

[1] *Sartor Resartus*, Book IV, Chap. IV.
[2] *Past and Present*, Book III, Chap. XII.

No treatment of this subject of work could have contemporary relevance without some reference to the burning topic of the incentive to work. In primitive man the main incentive is subsistence—man must work in order to eat; in civilized and especially urbanized man the issue is much more complicated, but the subsistence motive still persists when men work for wages with which to buy food and for profit, which also is related to subsistence. Can we eliminate the profit motive? Is service to the community the sole truly ethical motive? We shall have to pay attention to the new set-up of the Stakhanovite hierarchy or heroism of labour in Russia. We shall also have to look at the question of the "ca' canny" policy, as contrasted with the exploitation of the "go-getter", in both of whom the true motive of work seems to have been perverted. Can we encourage enterprise without permitting exploitation? Our present economic urgency, bordering on extremity, may lead us to develop a "work for work's sake" economy, or "work for export's sake" at all costs. We may also look at the danger inherent in the policy of full employment on which the whole complicated structure of social security rests, and the paraphernalia of propaganda and advertisement which may be called into being to sell the products we must produce in order to keep men at work in spite of the sales-resistance of those who do not really want or need what is produced. All these are vital and difficult questions which we cannot answer at this stage. But first let us look at the idea of work in Greek and Hebrew antiquity.

Chapter Nine

THE GREEK IDEA OF WORK

WE have to guard against very real danger in selecting one or two expressions of the genius of a people. For example, the thinking of Plato and Aristotle is not necessarily typical of the Greek "way of life"; in fact, we know that they both shared with Socrates a very critical attitude to many typical Greek ways of thinking and behaving. When we go to a writer like Hesiod, we find clues to typical Greek thinking on a subject like this.[1] In his *Works and Days*, the myth of the Golden Age finds fairly coherent expression, followed by other Ages of Silver, Bronze and Iron, in each of which a characteristic type of man was supposed to exist; a Golden Race in the Golden Age, under the rule of Kronos. Subsequent ages represented progressive degeneration. "At the beginning the generations of men lived on the earth far removed from evils of difficult toil and the painful diseases which have brought miseries upon mankind. . . . Men of the Golden Age used to live like gods, their souls were free from cares, from labour and from grief. . . . All good things were

[1] Even there we must remember how difficult it is to get a true insight into the attitude of a people, particularly a people so diverse as the Greeks. Their thinking may not represent accurately their "way of life". It is possible, for instance, that Zimmern, in his *Greek Commonwealth*, lays too much emphasis on the usages at Athens. We know how different was the culture of Athens from that of Sparta. We know also that city life was beginning to diverge from the usages of the countryside. And further we know something of the extent to which the simple life of the earlier ages had begun to degenerate, especially in the towns, by the time chroniclers attempted to describe it.

at their disposal. The fruitful earth gave them of herself fruits in abundance and in peace and tranquillity they used to share among themselves those good things in the midst of opulence."[1] Notice here how (1) men lived like gods; (2) as the gods were impassive, that meant no cares; (3) no toilsome work; (4) no grief; (5) the earth spontaneously provided their food and they shared this opulence (presumably without quarrelling). As degeneration set in, the gods "have hidden the livelihood of men". So they had to win their food by sweat, "in front of virtue have the deathless gods set sweat". Sickness and disease appeared. It is worth while noting how the word "*ponos*" means both hard work and hardship, and "*poneros*" comes to mean "a rogue". "Works" become "sinful works" (v. 124).[2]

Such views were not Hesiod's own invention. He was merely interpreting and making coherent current folk-lore and his attitude was the typically Greek way of looking at things. The ideal man was a gentleman and lived a life of ease, exempt from toil, care, hardship and illness; the inferior kind of man was subject to all these things. The more the world degenerated from the Golden Age, the more these undesirable elements came to preponderate. They were not natural to man in his essence, nor were they in themselves desirable.[3] Lucretius later adopted this pessimistic attitude to human life and emphasized how the earth as it decayed became more and more reluctant to yield its fruits, so that man's work was always becoming more toilsome and disagreeable: in the end he could not arrest this decay or his own constantly increasing wretchedness. Work to him also is a defect and the symbol of the doom of the creature man.

Against this attitude we must put the known facts of the

---

[1] *Works and Days*, Verses 90-91, 112, 113, 117-19.

[2] Cf. the *labor improbus* of the *Georgics* (I, 146), where the adjective like the Greek adjective translated "sinful" in Hesiod, v. 124, means "unbridled", "measureless", even "atrocious", not "sinful", in the narrowly moral sense. Note how in Latin "labor", like "ponos" in Greek, means both toil and pain.

[3] But note, "Work is no reproach: the reproach is idleness . . . whatever be thy lot, work is best . . .", v. 314. Cf. Eccles. 5: 18-20, and 2: 17-26.

common life in Athens and in Rome, as described in Zimmern, *The Greek Commonwealth*, particularly Chapters VII, VIII and IX, and Warde Fowler, *Social Life at Rome*, especially Chapters II and VII. In the more primitive times in both cities the number of slaves was small, the number of free craftsmen large and the social structures were built up in a most wholesome manner and based on the wise use of land. "The Greeks never recognized any distinction between a craft or 'trade' and a 'profession' ".[1] "There is no Greek word for 'Art' in the sense of fine art as distinguished from crafts and trades. This must be borne in mind when we read of Athenian devotion to Art and contempt of manual labour. They had not even the words to express such a thought. The term *banausos*, which does imply something of the sort, is strictly limited to such trades as mar body or soul or both. . . . The conventional view that Greek civilization provided for the culture of the few by relegating manual work to slave labour will not bear serious examination. Most Athenians were small farmers or small traders. On the other hand, the Greeks were too honest with themselves to ignore the fact that there were occupations inconsistent with the highest excellence, just as there are now. . . . It is the indoor and sedentary nature of some occupations which made them unfit for a free man."[2]

While democracy was a discovery of the Greeks, and the Greeks in their earlier days were democratic not only in the government of their city states, but democratic in their way of living, as Greek civilization developed, and they began to reflect on the meaning of life, it is true to say that Greek philosophical thinking on the subject is almost invariably aristocratic and hierarchical. In Plato's *Republic* the rulers are men of gold, whose function is contemplation. Plato has some difficulty in explaining how these philosophers are to be persuaded to undertake the arduous work of governing,

[1] Zimmern, *op. cit.*, p. 257.
[2] J. Burnet, *Plato's Euthyph-ro, Apology and Crito*, pp. 95-96.

which even in those simpler times looked dangerously like work (Book IV). Warriors or guardians are a race of silver, while the artisans are of bronze and must remain helots without citizen rights. They are an inferior type of man, condemned to slavery and incapable of the higher virtues. Their toil disqualifies them. The word used (by Aristotle) to describe this twist which disfranchises all hand-workers is *banausia*. (By the time of Aristotle the word had degenerated to mean the vulgarity of a mere labourer. He had become a menial.)

In fact Plato is so far carried away with his own logic, that he has to brand not merely the craftsman, because he has to work and works with raw materials and tools, but the poet, because he too works with tools and raw materials. He too is a kind of craftsman, only he does not make things nor even use them, but merely makes representations of things, which are imitations and not real.[1] Both the artist and the artisan are disqualified from the highest kind of life, which is pure contemplation. Plutarch even said that no young man of good birth could possibly desire to be a Phidias or a Polyclitus.[2] This is important, because it shows how disparagement of labour always inevitably means in the end disparagement of artistic expression, dependent as all such expression must be on some physical media. Representational art, according to Plato, is too far removed from reality. It is a copy of a copy (*Republic*, Book X).

This scorn for toil among the Greek thinkers is largely due to the institution of slavery, so fundamentally unjust.

As the number of slaves increased this scorn for work was accentuated. "It is not altogether impossible to understand whence arose, in decadent days, the false idea that the Greeks of the great age regarded manual labour as degrading; though it is still difficult to explain how, with the Parthenon

---

[1] Note that Plato does not include all art in this condemnation; not even all poetry is representational and so "imitative".

[2] Cf. "Who would care to be Phidias?" and the preference for the connoisseur as a greater man than the creator. See Zimmern, p. 271n.

before their eyes, men can believe so still."[1] The great achievements of Greek architecture were the product largely of free labour, as opposed to those of Egypt and Assyria, etc. "In truth they honoured manual work far more than we", says Zimmern,[2] though they honoured only such toil as contributed to some result that was artistically satisfying. Mere work for wages they abominated.[3]

Some men had the mentality of slaves and so the highest life for them was simply to obey. Aristotle admits that friendship is possible between a master and a slave, but that is because they are complementary elements in one social whole. Their human nature is fundamentally different: the master need not persuade the slave. (That would involve a recognition of a common reason.) Each type of man has its own peculiar excellence and the virtue of the master is not of the same kind as that of the slave. But the slave, though strictly not a member of the community, is by his domestic relation to his master given a status higher than is enjoyed by a cobbler in his workshop. "Our relations with inanimate objects do not admit of friendship or justice; nor our relations with a horse or an ox; nor our relations with a slave as such. For there is nothing in common between master and slave. The slave is a living tool; the tool is a lifeless slave. As a slave, then, his master's relations with him do not admit of friendship, but as a man they may: for there seems to be room for some kind of justice in the relations of any man to anyone that can participate in law and contract,—and if so, then for some kind of friendship, so far, that is to say, as he deserves the name man."[4] In the light of this we must qualify what Borne and Henry say: "In the worker, the artisan, the wisdom of antiquity was unable to recognize the man."[5] But we

[1] Zimmern, *op. cit.*, p. 270.
[2] *Ibid.*, p. 270.
[3] *Ibid.*, pp. 269, 270. One must keep Burnet's and Zimmern's facts before one to avoid the mistake of taking Plato and Aristotle as typical of all Greek thinking and of the "Greek way of life".
[4] *Nicomachean Ethics*, Book VIII: 11: 7. (Peters)
[5] *A Philosophy of Work*, p. 43.

can say that Greek thought finds it difficult to recognize that those who work with their hands are not disabled from full humanity and disqualified from citizenship by the indignity of handling tools and making things out of raw materials. "Work is a servile thing, because it forces upon the soul a resemblance to the matter which it works upon and modifies; it is human in proportion as it is the service by means of which a few persons are allowed the privilege of enjoying leisure. . . . The intoxication of disinterested knowledge which was the marvellous discovery of Hellas, caused it to disregard the eminent dignity of service."[1]

Contemplation to the Greeks and not merely to their philosophers is the highest kind of life, leisure is nobler than work, though we must remember that in Aristotle and others there is a very real and fundamental distinction between *energeia*, the kind of activity which man shares with the gods and which is involved even in contemplation, and *ponos*, which is the toil and drudgery of hard work. Strictly speaking, we cannot say of the Gods that they do or make anything.[2]

"Everything goes to prove the deliberate and universal scorn of work."[3] This is much too strong, and not strictly true even of later literary expressions. "In Sparta, the law forbade a citizen to take upon himself the servitude of any manual occupation."[4] At Thebes, shopkeepers could only become magistrates after ten years' retirement. But Herodotus said the Corinthians were exceptions to the universal scorn of mechanical arts among Greeks and barbarians alike. "They make much of their artisans."[5]

[1] Borne and Henry, *ibid.*, p. 43.
[2] *Nicomachean Ethics*, X, 8, Section 7-8. Cf. the treatment of "travail", as contrasted with "agir" and "action", as these can be applied to God, in Clavier, *Le Christianisme et Le Travail*, App. I. See also De Mam, *Joy in Work*, p. 66.
[3] Borne and Henry, *ibid.*, p. 43.
[4] *Op. cit.*, p. 31.
[5] *Ibid.*, p. 30.

Chapter Ten

THE HEBREW IDEA OF WORK

TO the Greeks the ethical ideal was a gentleman of leisure and serenity, who did not need to work with his hands. Work was an indignity, a disability, cutting a man off from God and degrading him among his fellows, below the level of true humanity and full citizenship. When Cleon, the leather-worker, became a power in politics at Athens this was supposed to be the *reductio ad absurdum* of all true order and decency.

The Romans made no great or distinctive contribution to the philosophy of work, or indeed to any philosophy.[1] They did not think much about work, they did it. Their contribution was in administration, in law, in affairs. For a real contribution to thought on the subject we have to wait for St. Augustine, whom we shall consider when we reach the dis-

[1] See, on this, W. Warde Fowler, *Social Life at Rome in the Age of Cicero*, especially pp. 43-44: "Cicero expresses this contempt for the artisan and trading classes in more than one striking passage. One, in his treatise on Duties, is probably paraphrased from the Greek of Panaetius, the philosopher who first introduced Stoicism to the Romans, and modified it to suit their temperament, but it is quite clear that Cicero himself entirely endorses the Stoic view. 'All gains made by hired labourers,' he says, 'are dishonourable and base, for what we buy of them is their labour, not their artistic skill: with them the very gain itself does but increase the slavishness of the work. All retail dealing too may be put in the same category, for the dealer will gain nothing except by profuse lying, and nothing is more disgraceful than untruthful huckstering. Again, the work of all artisans (*opifices*) is sordid; there can be nothing honourable in a workshop.' " Note on p. 44, after quoting Livy to the same effect, Warde Fowler draws attention to the close parallel of the English disdain of 'trade', which 'has only within the last century begun to die out'.

tinctively Christian idea of work. The Romans were very practical people, but with them as with the Greeks, it was probably the institution of slavery that was responsible for the loss of their simplicity and their ultimate deterioration.[1]

Let us turn to the Old Testament and in particular to the Book of Genesis, which is important for our purpose, whatever be our particular method of interpretation, whether it be treated as history or as vision. From the very first sentences it represents (1) God at work—that is to say, He is conceived as actively interested, concerned and responsible in human affairs. Indeed there is some ground for the reproach that the Hebrew thought of God from the beginning was of a worker God (the Demiurge).[2] (2) Verse 4a, of Chapter 2, marks the end of the first account of Creation, with the Sabbath rest. Notice its connection with Chapter 1, vv. 4, 10, 12, 18, 21, 25 and 31. In each case the Creator is represented as pausing after a further act of Creation and contemplating what He had made. The end of the Creation story gives us a further pause on the Seventh Day.[3] There is no suggestion that the Almighty has to wrestle with the hostile forces of Chaos, so that the work of Creation becomes toilsome, "as if work were a toil to God".[4] The rest of the Seventh Day is not through weariness. Creation is in each case by the Word "and God said". There is no manipulation of pre-existent matter by hand, as in the Babylonian myths and Plato's *Timaeus*, until we reach 5: 28, when the object of man's being put in the garden is stated "to replenish the earth and subdue it; and have dominion . . .". (3) In the second account of Creation, Chapter 2, vv. 4b, onwards,[5] two things are wanting (v. 5): (a) "moisture",[6] and (b) "a man to till the ground". These are supplied in vv. 6

---

[1] See Warde Fowler, *ibid.*, Chap. VII, especially pp. 230-36.
[2] Origen, *Contra Celsum*, c. 36.
[3] All this, to 2: 4a, belongs to the P tradition.
[4] Aug. *Civ. Dei.*, XI, 8.
[5] From here to the end of Chap. 4 is attributed to the J tradition.
[6] Cf. Chap. 1: 6, 7.

and 7. In vv. 8 and 9, "The Lord God planted a garden . . ."
Verses 10–14, rivers provide water for the garden "and the
lands beyond". In vv. 15–18 the man is put into the garden
to "dress it and to keep it", that is, to continue and co-
operate with the work of Creation already begun. Verses
16 and 17 set certain limitations upon man's life. Verse 18 is
a recognition of his loneliness. Verses 19–20, Adam is given
the prerogative of giving a name by which each living creature would be called, but none of these living creatures could
provide a mate for him. Verses 21–23, though Adam is
formed of the dust and the breath of God, woman is formed
from man and in v. 24 they become one flesh again in wed-
lock. In v. 25, idyllic, non-ethical conditions still prevail,
until, with Chapter 3, the serpent enters, is presumably
jealous of the woman's supremacy and excites her envy,
vv. 1–6. In Chapter 3, v. 7, the idyllic conditions have been
destroyed. Shame enters and we find man no longer willing
to commune with God in the cool of the day as before. Man
blames woman for his presumption and his fall. The woman
blames the serpent. A curse is put upon all three. Enmity
arises between the serpent and the woman. *The woman's
punishment is painful child-birth* and subjection to man, *the
man's punishment is to wring his livelihood from the earth on which
a curse has also been laid,* so that it will be reluctant to bring
forth food for him. It is interesting that the Hebrew word
for toil and pain in Chapter 3, vv. 16 and 17, is the same (see
RV and M). It is worth noting how in language after language the same word is used for toil and child-bearing,
e.g. "labour" and "travail".

Note how two things are apparently held together. (1)
Work is a thing to which man is called by the original intention of God, and it is the purpose for which man was set in
the world, but work in idyllic conditions, in partnership
with God, and interspersed with seasons of contemplation
and communion. There is no parallel in Hesiod to this. (2)
Work in its toilsome and harsh aspects is a punishment for

sin, the result of a curse set upon the earth and upon man and woman for their disobedience. Man was meant to be a gardener, but by reason of his sin he became a farmer, wringing his bread out of reluctant nature in the sweat of his brow, and shut out from the place where he could commune with God when he had done his day's work.

But, and here is a most delicate touch, to face this hard lot, the man and woman are thrust out, not clad only with the inadequate fig-leaf aprons they had woven in the first access of shame, but the Lord God made coats of skins and clothed them (3: 21). He did not give them the skins and say: "Make yourselves coats". We have here not merely the first lesson in manufacture, we have the story of the Prodigal Son in reverse, for we read that the Prodigal on his return was clothed in the best robe and here God prepares, provides and protects the man and woman whom He drives out, against the hardships and hazards of life in the world outside.

It is not impossible to weave these two thoughts together, and what we would get would be something like this. Creative work is the purpose of man's life and this he shares with God, as one made in His image. This work is not meant to be a hardship.[1] It only becomes so when, and in so far as, man by his sinfulness has interrupted the true natural order and run counter to God's will; i.e. the back-breaking and soul-destroying properties of much work are not in the original purpose of God. Work itself is a blessing and not a curse, but it is not meant to be the whole of life, the Sabbath was hallowed above the other days and Eden was to be both the place of man's work and of his communion with God. It is only a step from this to the Commandment: "Six days shalt thou labour and do all thy work, but the seventh day is the Sabbath of the Lord thy God. In it thou shalt not do any work . . ." (Exodus 20: 9–10).

It is easy to see how much farther Genesis takes us than

---

[1] "A Symbol for Punishment". De Man, *op. cit.*, p. 67.

Hesiod. A creating (and redeeming) God invites man to work creatively in and upon material created for personal, spiritual purposes. To such a view work as such is a privilege and assertion of kinship with God. Yet it is not meant to fill the whole picture of man's life. Other things have to be reckoned with and have room kept for them with sacred devotion, following the example of the Creator Himself. Such is the origin and importance of the Sabbath Rest.

A glance at a Concordance will show by the very frequency of mentions of work throughout the Old Testament that the Greek idea of the indignity of work has no place whatever there. (1) God is continually at work in the world and men are summoned by faith to consider the works of God (Job 37: 14 f.). (2) God is at work on behalf of man, in Providence (though the word is never used in this active and benevolent conception). (3) As man is created to work and in so doing to share in the nature of God, God appoints him his work and it is to be done "for the glory of God". There is no parallel to this in Greek thought. This idea is best developed, however, in the Apocryphal Ecclesiasticus, chapter 38. In the writer, Jesus ben Sirach, there is a strong Greek influence from his travel and up-bringing in Greek culture. Note in this chapter: (1) the honour given to the professional man (the doctor), who is the agent of the Creator, and (2) to the good craftsman, "wise in his work" and indispensable to the city (vv. 31, 32). *But* he "shall not be sought for in public counsel, nor sit high in the congregation: they shall not sit on the Judge's seat, nor understand the sentence of judgment: they cannot declare justice and judgment; and they shall not be found where parables are spoken. But they will maintain the state of the world, and (all) their desire is in the work of their craft" (vv. 33–34). "How can he get wisdom that holdeth the plough . . .?" (v. 25). Elsewhere we have a sentence which Paul echoes in 1 Corinthians 7: 20: "Trust in the Lord and abide in thy labour" (*Ecclus.* 11: 21).

131

Observe here how the typical Hebrew regard for the worker is tempered by the typical aristocratic Greek doctrine that manual work disables a man from exercising spiritual functions and sharing in the responsibilities of government and even in the privileges of citizenship. This is made even clearer in chapter 39. It is difficult to believe that verse 28 of chapter 38 is not a paraphrase of *banausia*, which is supposed to mean the deadening and disabling effect of sitting by a hot fire all day long, as the blacksmith did.[1]

It is not necessary to dwell on the frequent mentions, especially in the Wisdom Books, of diligence and acquired skill as commendable things, e.g. "to labour and to be content with that a man hath is a sweet hope" (Ecclus. 40: 18). The prudential morality of Proverbs has frequent exhortations to work, but except in the passage in Ecclus. 38, there is little if any trace of the Greek hauteur. Whereas the Greek ideal was a man of independent means, leisure and self-sufficiency, a gentleman, an ideal both ethical and aesthetic (a *kalokagathos*), the Hebrew ideal was of a man of much greater earnestness, an upright man of integrity with a stern sense of responsibility and duty, a just man in the severely ethical sense.

In case we should believe that all Greek thinking was of one type and all Hebrew thinking of another, we should remember that there is a humanist strain in certain Hebrew writings, as we have seen in Ecclesiasticus, and there was a strong ascetic strain, particularly in the Stoic contribution to Greek thinking, that was singularly attractive to the Romans with their *gravitas* and had a deep influence upon Roman thought and conduct. Indeed it was this Stoic ideal of conduct that was the nearest approach to a philosophy the Roman Republic and Empire ever had.

[1] Indeed it is very difficult to believe that the writer of this verse was not acquainted with Xenophon, *Oec.*, IV, 2, "the *locus classicus* for *banausia*" (Zimmern, *op. cit.*, p. 271n).

Chapter Eleven

WORK IN THE NEW TESTAMENT AND EARLY CHURCH

THERE is no theory of work in the recorded Gospels. But there is no theory of anything in the Gospels. Jesus was not concerned with philosophies or philosophers, but with plain men and women, earning their living, mostly in the sweat of their brows. Jesus never talked about the idea of work, He simply said: "My Father worketh hitherto and I work." "I must work the works of Him that sent Me, while it is day: the night cometh when no man can work" (John 9: 4). He was commissioned and "sent" to do a certain "work", and when He had finished it He said: "I have glorified Thee on the earth: I have finished the *work* which Thou gavest Me to do" (John 17: 4). It was His sense of "mission" which sustained and nourished His soul. When the disciples tried to persuade Him to eat He replied to their bewilderment: "I have meat to eat that ye know not of" (John 4: 32). "My meat is to do the will of Him that sent Me and to finish His work (John 4: 34). Here we get the most important principle: *to a man's soul a sense of mission is the sustaining thing that food is to the body*, a profoundly significant thought as regards vocation.[1]

Further, when He had fed the Five Thousand and the crowds were pressing round Him, He sees quite clearly that what they want is "bread from Heaven" (John 6: 31). That is bread without working for it. Jesus, taking them where

[1] See Ritschl, *Justification and Reconciliation*, p. 449.

they were—eager to break the entail by which bread would only follow upon work and must be earned by work—excited their curiosity. You must work to eat; very well, but you need more than bread for the body. "Man shall not live by bread alone" (Matt. 4: 4). Work for the bread that sustains without being consumed.[1]

But just when the crowd are keyed up on the edge of the discovery how to be able to repeat the miracle and draw their daily bread from Heaven, Jesus disappoints them. No effort can earn this bread or repeat the miracle—"This is the work of God, that ye believe on Him whom He hath sent" (John 6: 29). The gift of manna is the gift of the Messiah. "I am the bread of life . . ." (v. 35). Jesus has now led them so far away from work—wages—bread, that obviously they are too bewildered to understand, and the next verses to the end of the chapter drive home His teaching in words which must have seemed intolerable nonsense to most of the bystanders, but yet had the seeds of much fruitful meditation, especially after the Crucifixion. On any interpretation of the Fourth Gospel this will hold. People were jumping at the chance of bread without work and eager to learn how to make manna into daily bread; and Jesus leads them as He so often and so skilfully did from such obvious and immediate desires, into the deepest spiritual truths about God.

There is no injunction to work hard anywhere in the Gospels, but nowhere is there any question that work is the inevitable lot of man. A moment's reflection will show how far we are, in the whole story from John the Baptist onwards, from the Greek hauteur about the craftsman's *banausia*. There is scarcely a single character in the New Testament picture, till we reach St. Paul, that Plato and Aristotle would have honoured with more than a passing glance. Perhaps Socrates would have been different, but no

[1] Note here the interesting parallel with the living water in John 4: 5-15, where the woman wants water so that first she need never be thirsty, and second she be spared the labour of coming to the well.

man knows how different. Jesus, we believe, spent most of His life at the carpenter's bench, and St. Paul worked as a tent-maker to avoid being dependent on anyone—a fact of which St. Augustine makes much in his *De Opere Monachorum*. Every Hebrew boy was supposed to learn a trade, not merely as a matter of economic prudence, but, as the Talmud says: "It is well to add a trade to your studies if you would be free from sin."

The matter is much more fundamental than the new dignity of labour, that has its origins in the carpenter's shop, the cottage at Nazareth, and current Jewish practices. The very Incarnation itself, "The Word was made flesh", swept away by a supreme act of transcendence by humiliation the Greek idea that the material world itself was the source of evil and the prison of the soul. By removing the stigma from the material world that it was itself, as the source of evil, essentially evil, the reproach was also removed both from the craftsman and from the artist, that by dabbling in material things they were debasing the purity of their souls. That is why both arts and crafts have found their inspiration in the Incarnation story, for both are in a sense incarnations of spirit in matter and derive much of their significance to us from the fact that Incarnation is God's way in dealing with the world, and with man. He is the supreme artist, and the artist in representing, "figuring forth", spiritual ideas through material media, is treading in the footsteps of God. Possibly only with the help of the artist shall we succeed in restoring the true spirit of joy in work, recovering the true meaning of work as creative production. Indeed to-day many artists and craftsmen are looking to religion to interpret for them that which each is seeking to express in his own medium.

"No pagan philosopher could produce an adequate aesthetic, simply for lack of a right theology," says Dorothy Sayers.[1] A discussion of the meaning of art is beyond our

[1] *Our Culture* (ed. Demant), p. 53.

present purpose, but Dorothy Sayers is not the only person to see in a Gospel of Incarnation and Atonement the true inspiration for genuine art, which is neither mere entertainment nor mere ethical propaganda, but somehow as closely related to reality as is faith itself.

When we turn to St. Paul, we find first of all his own example. He worked with his own hands, so that he would not be chargeable to anyone. He exhorts new converts in an early letter—"that ye study to be quiet, and to do your business, and to work with your hands, as we commanded you" (1 Thess. 4: 11). He dismisses idleness in a peremptory word: "If any will not work, neither let him eat" (2 Thess. 3: 10).[1] The whole passage on 2 Thessalonians is instructive:

> He (Paul) neither regards it (work) in the spirit of Gn. 3: 19 as an unfortunate necessity brought about by the Fall, nor in the modern Christian sense, as something to be done to the glory of God. He dissociates himself from the general Greek view, which regarded manual labour as the vocation of slaves and not of gentlemen, and supports the Jewish rabbinical insistence on the dignity of hard work. His own training as a rabbi had necessarily included an apprenticeship to a trade—despite his father's probable affluence—and this no doubt coloured his outlook. The Talmud teaching is crystal clear—that service to the community in the most menial task was honourable, though the Wisdom scribes had inclined to the Greek view. Here, however, Paul is offering no general theory. Other facets of his attitude to work appear in other references—as a means of helping the needy (Eph. 4: 28), or to keep people out of mischief (1 Thess. 4: 11). In this case all he is concerned to stress is that it is a right and proper thing for a Christian man to be self-supporting and not to live off the community. He assumes that employment is available, and takes no account of such a phenomenon as enforced idleness in an industrial society.[2]

[1] Cf. Hesiod: "Hunger is altogether meet companion of the man who will not work. At him are Gods and men wroth . . . whoso liveth in idleness is like in temper to the stingless drones, which in idleness waste and devour the labour of the bees." (*Work and Days*, pp. 302–6)

[2] *The Epistles to the Thessalonians* (Moffatt Commentary, William Neil, p. 197).

For all his insistence on the importance of work, St. Paul knew that work could never earn or win salvation. The supposed controversy about faith and works in Romans, and again in the Epistle of St. James, need not detain us, as it is not entirely relevant to this subject. Suffice it to say that Paul himself, while strenuously and consistently denying that a man's earnestness and diligence could earn his salvation, yet accepts and inculcates diligence and moral earnestness as the inevitable results of an experience of salvation. As he puts it in Philippians 2: 12 and 13: "Work out (*katergazesthe*) your own salvation with fear and trembling, for it is God which worketh (*energōn*) in you both to will and to do (*energein*) of his good pleasure", where "work" and "work out" are deliberately contrasted with admirable theological and ethical effect.

We cannot blame St. Paul for the teaching of 2 Peter. Curiously enough the introduction to that remarkable little book has the un-Pauline phrase "that hath called us to glory and virtue" (2 Peter 1: 3), and goes on "giving all diligence, add to your faith virtue . . . give diligence to make your calling and election sure: for if ye do these things, ye shall never fall" (v. 10). The last phrase is taken by supporters of the Max Weber thesis as the *leit-motif* of the Calvinist-Puritan, who devotes himself to business with a convinced sense of vocation, and treats his success in the world of affairs as a proof or verification of his standing with God— a very dangerous doctrine.

We have already discussed in Part I, Chapter Three, the development of the "two-standard" doctrine of Christian morality, and the way in which this doctrine deprived daily life of the sense of vocation we see in the New Testament and the earliest documents, and sterilized religious earnestness within the monasteries. We need only refer to the passages from the Epistle *Ad Diognetum* (p. 41) and from Eusebius' *Demonstratio Evangelica* (pp. 42–3). For an excellent example of the way in which the new spirit transformed all

137

old relationships we have only to read the Epistle to Philemon, where St. Paul apparently acquiesces in the institution
of slavery, yet so completely transforms it by the new fellowship of faith which now linked Onesimus and Philemon to
Paul, and therefore to one another, that the master-slave
relationship can no longer be maintained. The story of the
influence of the new faith on the institution of slavery, by
which the whole social structure continued for hundreds of
years to be supported, is instructive even when it is humiliat-
ing. The new brotherhood made slavery an anachronism,
but it was only the slow growth of a wage system that made
it possible finally to abolish slavery, if it has been abolished.
No mere crusade could ever have succeeded in getting rid
of it, there had to be some better way possible. The mere
impact of a new idea can seldom get rid of an abuse, the new
idea has in some sense to clothe itself in the institutional
clothing of that which it is trying to supplant, to be translated into the idiom of the appropriate "order".

Though St. Paul may seem unduly conservative, he yet
enunciates principles that changed the whole aspect of work:

"Servants, be obedient to them that are your masters
according to the flesh, with fear and trembling, in singleness
of your heart, as unto Christ; not with eye service, as men-
pleasers; but as the servants of Christ, doing the will of God
from the heart; with good will doing service, as to the Lord,
and not to men: knowing that whatsoever good thing any
man doeth, the same shall he receive of the Lord, whether he
be bond or free. And, ye masters, do the same things unto
them, forbearing threatening: knowing that your Master
also is in heaven; neither is there respect of persons with
him" (Eph. 6: 5–9). If we take along with this the first four
verses of the same chapter, and read them in the light of
the verses from 1 Corinthians 7, already discussed in Part I,
Chapter Two, we get quite coherent and most valuable
guidance as to motive and conduct; and in the Epistle *Ad
Diognetum* we see how revolutionary the change was that

conversion made. The new man behaved in a new way. Dependence no longer constituted inferiority, even the status of a slave ceased to be a disability, brotherhood was a fact, and a new motive transformed every task. Onesimus, the "unprofitable" slave, became the "profitable" brother beloved, for whom Paul bespoke all the privileges of "partnership" (v. 17). As both he and his master were spiritual sons of the Apostle they would not deny to one another the relationship of brotherhood. The new spiritual relationship brought a new economic status, so that it was not long before it became incongruous for a Christian to retain a Christian brother as his slave.

The whole story cannot yet be told, for it is not yet complete. It was in 1727 that the Bishop of London wrote to the Masters and Mistresses of the Southern American Colonies:

"Christianity and the embracing of the Gospel does not make the least alteration in civil property or in any of the duties that belong to civil relations, but in all these respects it continues Persons just in the same State as it found them. The Freedom which Christianity gives is freedom from the bondage of Sin and Satan and from the Dominion of Men's Lusts and Passions and inordinate Desires; but as to their outward condition, whatever that was before, whether bond or free, their being baptized and becoming Christians makes no manner of change in them".[1]

Here we see how 1 Corinthians 7 can be used, along with Romans 13, to justify quietism and inculcate docility. At the present day, Scripture is quoted in South Africa in support of the permanent subjection of the black to the white races. Indeed there are paternalistic strands in the Christian tradition which have throughout the history of our era been used to justify pretty doubtful race and class relationships. But though the history of the influence of religion on slavery, for instance, has been a mixed one (slavery and annexation have

[1] Quoted by Richard Niebuhr, *Social Sources of Denominationalism*, p. 249.

on occasion been justified as methods of evangelism!), neither the Church nor the world since the time of Christ has been able to escape from the new principle, that dependence is no indignity (in the community any more than in the family, see Eph. 6), that need does not imply inferiority. In fact some of the most enlightened provisions of modern legislation, e.g. those removing the stigma of poverty, may be claimed as attempts to live up to the New Testament standards.

The slave once converted, worked for his master, even his heathen master, as entrusted by God with his work and responsible to Him for the way he did it, "from the heart". Onesimus now justified his name, and could no longer be treated on Aristotelian principles as a mere chattel. The Roman Empire had long ago been forced by its need for capable administrators to give a status to the freed-man, because he often showed himself worthy of responsibility and capable of leadership: much more the Church, which quite early had among its leaders slaves and former slaves. Though we know that such slaves and freed-men composed a considerable portion of the believers, there is no grave in the catacombs below Rome with an inscription recording that the deceased was a slave. In the sight of God, in the fellowship of the Church, and in the presence of death, such distinctions became irrelevant.

The motive of work was changed, and a revolution more drastic than any crusade against slavery had been begun. It has proceeded throughout the centuries ever since; there is no prospect that it has reached finality, or ever will. It fastened on the institution of slavery and so transformed it that the institution, though in New Testament times taken as the basis of society, being inherently incapable of redemption, had to go. In Europe slavery gave way to serfdom, which though it stereotyped inferiority, yet did give some status and security to the worker. With the economic changes around the opening of the Renaissance-Reformation era, the serf relationship in turn began to give way to a wage basis. This too has its ethical advantages and disadvantages; it gained liberty for the wage earner at the cost of his security, and emancipated him from a bondage which still gave a certain status and belonging, now lost in our nondescript aggregations of men in towns and factories.

We cannot do more than indicate these long vistas of economic history. The new spirit that entered men's work when they came to treat it as a stewardship from God, a vocation, came too late to save the Roman Empire, as an Empire. Perhaps there were elements in that empire which made its doom inevitable. By the time of St. Augustine the main emphasis and loyalty of Christianity had been changed from the duties of citizenship to those of the City of God.

There are those who see in the rise of monasticism the creation of a divided loyalty and the deflection of Christian devotion from the practical duties of citizenship to a self-stultifying piety. Others see in the creation of the monasteries a wise provision to maintain the purity of the faith and resist the shock of the break-up of the Roman Empire, a break-up which was inevitable in any case.

Very few would to-day echo the words of R. L. Stevenson, who, even when he reacted most strongly against his stern Calvinist upbringing, could not rid himself of its activism, as here in *Our Lady of the Snows*:

> And ye, O brethren, what if God,
> When from Heav'n's top He spies abroad,
> And sees on this tormented stage
> The noble war of mankind rage:
> What if His vivifying eye,
> O monks, should pass your corner by?
> For still the Lord is Lord of might;
> In deeds, in deeds, He takes delight;
> The plough, the spear, the laden barks,
> The field, the founded city, marks;
> He marks the smiler of the streets,
> The singer upon garden seats;

141

He sees the climber in the rocks;
To Him, the shepherd folds his flocks.
For those He loves that underprop
With daily virtues Heaven's top,
And bear the falling sky with ease,
Unfrowning caryatides.
Those He approves that ply the trade,
That rock the child, that wed the maid,
That with weak virtues, weaker hands,
Sow gladness on the peopled lands,
And still with laughter, song and shout,
Spin the great wheel of earth about.

But ye?—O ye who linger still
Here in your fortress on the hill,
With placid face, with tranquil breath,
The unsought volunteers of death,
Our cheerful General on high
With careless looks may pass you by.

In the medieval system with its feudal structure we see the
Greek *banausia* over again, but in its patriarchal set-up the
serf, though he did not matter much, had a sense of belonging which the Greek slave could seldom have; and in feudalism work had a religious motive, though the full sense of
vocation was reserved for the Call to "the religious life" in
the monastery. Every rank of life was supposed to have its
religious sanction and justification, but the whole ecclesiastical feudal structure of the medieval synthesis exhibits many
of the features of the Greek aristocratic ideal. It was not long
before special vices began to appear among the rather inbred
monkish communities, especially where the monastic life
took the form of a cult of the divine with no idea of service
of mankind (e.g. *accidie*). "The fourth, fifth and sixth centuries of our era witnessed a remarkable series of efforts to
bring the monastic life into close kinship with the secular.
It is difficult to exaggerate the courage and the conviction
of a Church which thus set out to use the weapons of discipline, not to repress open wickedness, but to prevent

142

those who were universally regarded as most saintly from becoming righteous overmuch."[1]

In 515 A.D., St. Benedict formulated his famous Rule, which became the model for most monastic foundations in western Europe. In that Rule, Benedict, who was a great reformer, put work and prayer, activity and contemplation, in their proper perspectives, or at least tried to do so. In all Benedictine monasteries, and the other Orders which were offshoots from the Benedictines, like the Cistercians, there was a vigorous daily programme of work. We know something of the debt civilization owed to the monks, not merely for their evangelizing zeal, but for their skill in husbandry, and even in the crafts, as well as their contribution to learning, by copying out and preserving all manner of documents, both sacred and profane.

There were certain kinds of work monks were not supposed to do. Agriculture and the crafts were permitted and enjoined, but not commerce or finance.[2]

As the Orders increased in wealth, the distinction between the permitted and the forbidden grew difficult to maintain, and as the feudal structure grew more complicated, it was more and more necessary for the administrators to be educated men. Hence the authority and influence of the Church increased, and more and more power fell into the hands both of the "secular" and of the "regular" clergy, i.e. those entrusted with pastoral duties and those living in community under a Rule. The fact that ordained persons were not supposed to fight led to much land falling into clerical administration, which in turn frequently led to ownership, till the Church owned most of the best land. The abuses so engendered were principally responsible for the Reformation.

[1] K. E. Kirk, *The Vision of God*, p. 257.
[2] "All religions are of the same condition with monks as regards their entire dedication to the divine service, the observance of the essential vows of religion, *and abstinence from secular business*". Aquinas, *Summa*, II, ii, Q, CLXXXVIII, Art. II, Para. 3. (*My italics*)

The manuals of Church history deal fully with the rise, importance, decline, and fall of the monastic movement. Generally speaking, the work of the monastery was intended (1) for subsistence and (2) for its antiseptic value in communities whose primary aim was worship and contemplation. Experience soon proved that a community sooner or later goes sour unless it does some wholesome extraverted work together. But you will observe how far we have travelled from St. Paul in 1 Corinthians 7: Stay in your status or job and make it a calling; and from 2 Peter: use it and transform it by your consecrated diligence. Hence in feudalism the Greek aristocratic hauteur about work not merely persisted, it was the prevailing attitude. The gently bred might and must fight. The knight boasted that he need not and did not work. The serf remained disabled and disenfranchised by his *banausia*. The monk shut himself away from all that, though usually dominating both knight and serf, but "religion" too was shut up in seclusion. The work-a-day world lacked emancipating and transforming vision and a sense of vocation, the practice of religion in a vacuum became rarified, introspective, effeminate and corrupt. The city of Cecrops languished, and the city of God was not built.[1]

St. Francis of Assisi was only one of many who tried to restore and purify monastic life, corrupted by wealth and power, and restore the religious significance of daily work. The Little Brethren were pledged to work as one of the elementary conditions of the simple life that Francis restored, and the distinctive obligations of the Third Order that he founded have been described thus by Sabatier: "To do with joy the duties of their calling; to give a holy inspiration to the slightest actions; to find in the infinitely littles of existence, things apparently the most commonplace, parts of a divine work; to keep pure from all debasing interest; to use things as not possessing them, like the ser-

[1] See Marcus Aurelius, *Meditations*, IV, 23.

vants in the parable who would soon have to give account of the talents committed to them. . . ."[1] The very conception of the Third Order, in which consecration did not mean seclusion from the world, but redeeming transformation of the secular by the sacred through those who were called to a religious life, but not to monkish apartness—this conception itself, as incarnated in the sacred simplicity of Francis himself, revived the lingering belief that religion must find its perfection in secular life and not apart from it. Elsewhere Sabatier says: "The Brothers, after entering upon the Order, were to continue to exercise the calling which they had when in the world, and if they had none they were to learn one. For payment they were to accept only the food that was necessary for them, but in case that was insufficient they might beg. In addition they were naturally permitted to own the instruments of their calling."[2] "This obligation to work with the hands . . . was destined hardly to survive St. Francis. . . . To it is due in part the original character of the first generation of the Order."[3] It is not too much to say that with St. Francis, almost as with Jesus Himself, the absolute seemed to enter the relativities of history in a disconcerting way.

But it was not till the Reformation that the centre of gravity was shifted from the monk, as the standard or ethical ideal, to the godly and industrious householder, and the doctrine of the "Calling" (*Beruf*) revived certain features of Pauline thinking once more. Calvin's treatment in *The Institutes*, Book III, Chapter X, Sections 1–6, ushers in a new era.

---

[1] Aug. Sabatier, *Life of St. Francis of Assisi*, p. 268.
[2] *Op. cit.*, p. 125. Cf. St. Francis' Will: "*firmiter volo quod omnes laborent*".
[3] *Ibid*.

Chapter Twelve

THE DOCTRINE OF VOCATION AS RESTORED BY CALVIN
AND LUTHER

IF it be true that under the influence of the "two-standard"
doctrine the new motive and dynamic brought into daily
life by Christ was diverted into the seclusion of "religion",
narrowly conceived as a way of life which "abstained from
secular business", it is to the Reformers we must turn for
the recovery of the sense that the Call of God could be best
heard and best obeyed in the due performance of the duties
of the secular "calling". The centre of gravity was shifted
from an other-worldliness that showed itself in a "cloistered
and sequestered virtue" to the wholesome disciplines of
household and market-place. We shall discuss later how perhaps the market-place has come to occupy the centre of the
picture formerly occupied by the Church, throwing the
whole picture as much out of perspective as it formerly was
distorted by the "two-standards" theory. Let us put down
the most important passage from Calvin's *Institutes* alongside one or two typical utterances of Luther's:

> The last thing to be observed is, that the Lord enjoins every
> one of us, in all the actions of life, to have respect to our own
> calling. He knows the boiling restlessness of the human mind,
> the fickleness with which it is borne hither and thither, its
> eagerness to hold opposites at one time in its grasp, its am-
> bition. Therefore, lest all things should be thrown into con-
> fusion by our folly and rashness, he has assigned distinct duties
> to each in the different modes of life. And that no one may

presume to overstep his proper limits, he has distinguished the different modes of life by the name of callings. Every man's mode of life, therefore, is a kind of station assigned him by the Lord, that he may not be always driven about at random. So necessary is this distinction, that all our actions are thereby estimated in his sight, and often in a very different way from that in which human reason or philosophy would estimate them . . . in everything the call of the Lord is the foundation and beginning of right action. He who does not act with reference to it will never, in the discharge of duty, keep the right path. He will sometimes be able, perhaps, to give the semblance of something laudable, but whatever it may be in the sight of man, it will be rejected before the throne of God; and besides, there will be no harmony in the different parts of his life. Hence, he only who directs his life to this end will have it properly framed; because, free from the impulse of rashness, he will not attempt more than his calling justifies, knowing that it is unlawful to overleap the prescribed bounds. He who is obscure will not decline to cultivate a private life, that he may not desert the post at which God has placed him. Again, in all our cares, toils, annoyances, and other burdens, it will be no small alleviation to know that all these are under the superintendence of God. The magistrate will more willingly perform his office, and the father of a family confine himself to his proper sphere. Every one in his particular mode of life will, without repining, suffer its inconveniences, cares, uneasiness, and anxiety, persuaded that God has laid on the burden. This, too, will afford admirable consolation, that in following your proper calling, no work will be so mean and sordid as not to have a splendour and value in the eye of God.[1]

Luther on Vocation in Daily Life:

What you do in your house is worth as much as if you did it up in heaven for our Lord God. For what we do in our calling here on earth in accordance with His word and command He counts as if it were done in heaven for Him[2]. . . . Therefore we should accustom ourselves to think of our position and work as sacred and well-pleasing to God, not on account of the position and the work, but on account of the word and faith

[1] *Institutes*, Book III, Chap. X, Sec. 6. (In the first edition the *Institutes* closed with this section).
[2] *Works* (Erlanger. ed.), Vol. V, p. 102.

147

from which the obedience and the work flow. No Christian should despise his position and life if he is living in accordance with the word of God, but should say, "I believe in Jesus Christ, and do as the ten commandments teach, and pray that our dear Lord God may help me thus to do." That is a right and holy life, and cannot be made holier even if one fast himself to death.[1] . . . It looks like a great thing when a monk renounces everything and goes into a cloister, carries on a life of asceticism, fasts, watches, prays, etc. . . . On the other hand, it looks like a small thing when a maid cooks and cleans and does other housework. But because God's command is there, even such a small work must be praised as a service of God far surpassing the holiness and asceticism of all monks and nuns. For here there is no command of God. But there God's command is fulfilled, that one should honour father and mother and help in the care of the home.[2]

Calvin's treatment, in the whole of Chapter Ten, which has been described as "extraordinarily narrow"[3] is very suggestive. Our "station" is no matter of accident or fate, but is appointed by God. Our conduct is determined by and relative to our station, as so appointed, giving us a very different standard of values from the standards of reason or philosophy. Duty then is to walk in the path so determined by God. A man who does so will find "harmony in the different parts of his life", as well as finding his own proper place among his fellows as intended by God. No one and nothing "in his calling" can be insignificant, and our attitude to suffering as well as to the opportunities and necessities of daily life is transformed when we consider ourselves under the personal care of God, whose Providence extends to the circumstances of our daily lives as well as to the salvation of our souls.

Elsewhere Calvin shows what he thinks of ambition: "Thus we see how pestilential a plague ambition is, from which envy springs up, and afterwards perfidy and cruelty."[4]

[1] *Ibid.*
[2] *Ibid.*, p. 100.
[3] J. G. Matheson, *Scottish Journal of Theology*, March, 1949, p. 55.
[4] Lecture on Daniel 6.

Faith delivers us from this inordinate element in human nature and teaches us that "all things work together for good to them that love God, who are the called according to His purpose" (Romans 8: 28).

Luther's teaching is a very close parallel to Calvin's, and to much the same effect. But Luther, as we saw in Part I, Chapter Three, is forced to make a dangerous distinction between the Godward aspects of vocation, in which all are, as individual persons, equally sinners, and no one is superior or inferior to anyone else, but all alike are recipients of Grace, and the manward aspects. In our relationships to our neighbours, the "offices" and "worldly or secular station" our lives are governed by law, and privilege, authority and inequality prevail. To Luther God deals with souls by Grace, but with the world by law. He refuses to allow law to reign in the purely spiritual world—that, he says, is the mistake Rome made—and we are left a little doubtful how Grace operates through law in the various secular vocations or "stations" of life in the world, in the family, in the State-relationships, and even in the ecclesiastical sphere of the ministry in its various forms. So Lutheranism, in trying to get rid of the relationship of mutual exclusiveness between sacred and secular, defined as they too often were against one another, was faced with and even helped to create a new antithesis between the private dealing of the soul with God in Grace and faith on the one hand, and on the other the behaviour of men with one another and the social structures in which they seek to embody their ideals not merely of justice, but of Grace active in the common life.

Luther finds in his distinction between the "*christlicher Stand*" and the "*weltlicher Stand*" the means of distinguishing between the senses in which all men are equal and those in which they are necessarily in need of Grace.[1] In the sight of men "no one can be regarded simply as a private person,

[1] "All stations are so made that they tend to service." Luther, quoted by P. S. Watson, *S.J.T.*, Dec., 1949, p. 370.

for everyone has a definite place in society, in relation to others. Here, therefore, the stations, offices, and vocations of the Law have their place, and everyone is a *Weltperson* and *Amtsperson*, a public person and office-bearer, invested with the privileges and responsibilities of his station. These he must accept and fulfil as his vocation, as commanded by God, neither neglecting the responsibilities nor using the privileges for his own ends."[1]

"No station in life, as Luther sees it, can be regarded as divinely ordained and a true vocation, unless it involves real service to others, and it is interesting to note that he condemns the usurer on ultimately the same grounds as the monk, since the disservice done to men by the taking of usury far outweighs the service rendered by a loan."[2]

Luther creates new difficulties, some of which dog Lutherism and indeed Protestantism to this day, especially the accentuated distinction between public and private capacities, which tended to encourage quietism and at the same time and for the same reason political (and economic) "realism" or "power-politics". Hence arose the unfortunate liaison between Lutheranism and Machiavellianism which has done so much mischief to Europe.[3]

Some of these difficulties were not long in showing themselves, as both Calvin and Luther found out when they confronted the secular powers, now no longer hostile but professing Reformed principles, only just emancipated from priestly dictation, unwilling to be dictated to from the pulpit, and obviously unable to usher in the Kingdom of God in Geneva, or the German towns and states. We know the troubles Knox had, not merely with Mary and her supporters, but with the Lords of the Congregation. We know what happened to most of the possessions of the pre-Reformation Church, and the indignation felt by the Reformers, when

[1] P. S. Watson, *ibid.*, p. 374.
[2] *Ibid.*, p. 373.
[3] See Figgis, *From Gerson to Grotius*, Lecture III.

they were confronted by Anabaptists and other sectaries, claiming the same liberty of non-conformity in the new Church and State that the Reformers had won for themselves against the Roman Church and feudal state. All these complicated issues are matters of history, but what concerns us particularly was that a new spirit was abroad, the moral earnestness that inevitably followed upon true living faith was now no longer sequestered and sterilized, but thrust like leaven into the world of affairs, often with unexpected results. And as we saw earlier the Renaissance and Reformation each so fertilized the other that a new era in history began. In that era diligence in work, devotion and faithfulness in one's calling, came to have an importance and to play a part that had been little better than a dream before.

It may be true that the difference that soon developed between Lutheranism and Calvinism was that between serving God *in vocatione*, interpreted in a more or less quietist sense in Lutheranism, or *per vocationem*, a much more thorough and activist attitude as in Calvinism.[1] We shall revert to this later, and proceed to discuss in the next chapter the influence of Protestantism on secular affairs, one of the burning points of ethical and historical controversy at the moment.

[1] See Flew, *The Idea of Perfection*, p. 252, with reference to Max Weber, *The Protestant Ethic*, p. 215, and Troeltsch, *The Social Teaching*, II, 576-691.

Chapter Thirteen

PROTESTANTISM AND THE SECULAR CALLING

IT is now over forty years since Max Weber wrote his famous essay on the relations of capitalism to the Protestant Ethic. In those forty years the subject has become vastly more important, and a large literature has arisen around it, in German, French, and English. Talcott Parsons, in his translation of Weber's essay, *The Protestant Ethic and the Spirit of Capitalism*,[1] gives a short list of some of the more important works and essays dealing with the subject, and the list has grown considerably longer since. Tawney's book, *Religion and the Rise of Capitalism*, has now appeared in very cheap reprints in Great Britain and in the U.S.A., and "the Weber thesis" in its original form, or more likely in Tawney's somewhat modified form, has become part of the mental currency of the man in the street, who in many cases has been persuaded that the "spirit of Capitalism" owes its origin to the Reformation, though Max Weber is careful never to say so in so many words.

Further, in the last forty years, the march of events has quickened interest in the relations of our economic system to its spiritual foundations. The neo-Thomists argue that our present international and economic malaise is the inevitable nemesis of the divisive forces released and produced by the Reformation, and advocate a return to the supposed spiritual unity of the medieval system.[2] The left-wing secu-

[1] Allen and Unwin, 1930, p. 4 f.
[2] See, for example, Jacques Maritain, Christopher Dawson and Fanfani, *Catholicism Protestantism and Capitalism*.

larists are more than willing to agree that capitalism has its roots in religious ideas—it is not a natural growth, but "a crass construction of the Calvinist mind"—and therefore they condemn its ideology as based on illusion. For Max Weber's thesis reverses what Marxist "realists" maintain to be the true order of events, by which economic forces and pressures produce social and religious ideas and institutions, instead of the other way round.[1]

If we agree with Tawney that Weber's thesis means that "Capitalism was the social counterpart of Calvinist theology",[2] then those who believe that capitalism has led us to disaster maintain that Protestantism is doomed with the decay of its inevitable sociological and economic embodiment. They point to the helplessness of the modern world in face of economic problems and war, and foretell the speedy end of the Reformation era.[3] From both sides Protestantism is assailed; and both parties make use of the Weber thesis. The left-wing arraign the Reformation because in producing capitalism it reversed the true order of history according to Karl Marx; and the Romanists, because it is responsible for the present "anarchy" in economics and international relationships, and for the prevailing materialism and secularism. It is therefore most necessary to subject Weber's thesis to analysis, all the more because the doctrine of vocation is bound to become more and more prominent in the near future both in ethics and in theology.

Naumann says that the religious appreciation of the secular callings is "an achievement of the Reformation".[4] Troeltsch proves the contrary, and Holl and others have shown how in the Mystics and in Aquinas, so far as theory

[1] To Marx Protestantism is essentially a bourgeois religion, *Das Kapital*, I, Chap. 27.
[2] Foreword to Weber's *The Protestant Ethic* (Eng. tr.), p. 2.
[3] Fanfani, after declaring repeatedly that "the Catholic ethos is anti-capitalistic" (pp. 143, 149, 151, 153, 159), claims that Catholicism is "looking forward to the time when it (capitalism) should give place to a corporative organization of society" (*op. cit.*, pp. 142, 159).
[4] In *Die Religion in Geschichte und Gegenwart* (R.G.G.), I, p. 1061.

went, and in the Guilds in practice, the later Middle Ages were struggling to express the idea.[1]

But it was only when Luther and Calvin revived the doctrine of the spiritual priesthood of all believers that a true and complete doctrine of "secular vocation" became possible.[2] Indeed, the doctrine of secular vocation is the necessary counterpart of the doctrine of the spiritual priesthood of all believers, as it is also of the doctrine of election itself.

Luther's use of words in his translation of the Bible is most interesting and important in this connection, but a discussion of it would be too technical.[3] The main point for our purpose is that Luther, in deposing the monk from his former position as the ideal of a Christian man, and putting the good householder in his place, changed the whole emphasis of Christian ethics, and gave a new start to the history of Europe.

> Neither the predominantly Catholic peoples nor those of classical antiquity have possessed any expression of similar connotation for what we know as a calling (in the sense of a life-task, a definite field in which to work), while one has existed for all predominantly Protestant peoples. . . . In its modern meaning the word (*Beruf*=calling) comes from the Bible translations, through the spirit of the translator, not that of the original. . . . After that it speedily took on its present meaning in the everyday speech of all Protestant peoples, while earlier not even a suggestion of such a meaning could be found in the secular literature of any of them, and even, in religious writings, so far as I can ascertain, it is only found in one of the German mystics whose influence on Luther is well known. Like the meaning of the word, the idea is new, a product of the Reformation.[4]

Luther's rediscovery of the Biblical meaning of "vocation" or

[1] Troeltsch, *Social Teaching in the Christian Churches*, I, p. 292, etc.; cf. Calhoun, *God and the Common Life*, p. 253. Fanfani, *op cit.*, pp. 201 and 160: "No one now denies that it (the advent of capitalism) took place before the Reformation and among Catholics."

[2] See Calhoun, *op. cit.*, p. 21.

[3] See Weber, *op. cit.*, pp. 79, 204-11; and Holl, *Die Aufsatze*, I, pp. 213-19.

[4] Weber, *op. cit.*, p. 79 f.; but cf. Fanfani, *passim*. With Weber's contribution here we do not altogether agree.

"calling" had revolutionary consequences. In the Middle Ages it was only the monk and the priest who had a divine vocation, not the layman. The idea of the *homo religiosus* being, by his divine vocation, the apex of the social scale dominated the whole of the structure of feudal society, culminating in the Pope and—at the other extreme—the peasant in an almost slave-like abasement. He, of course, had no divine vocation; this was the exclusive privilege of the *homines religiosi*. It was a direct consequence of Luther's rediscovery of the New Testament message that every Christian, whether a priest, a monk, a king or a housemaid, being called into the service of God, may look at the work he or she is doing as a divine calling or vocation. There is nothing "low" about the work of a housemaid. It is just as "high" as reading the mass or the breviary. It does not matter what you do, provided that whatever you do is done as a divine service to the glory of God.

By this new idea of calling or vocation the fatal dilemma is removed: the choice is between the highest valuation of the spiritual with a consequent devaluation of the economic physical work, or the removal of this dualism on the basis of a merely materialistic economy. If all work is divine service, it is ennobled by this highest calling. The difference in value no longer lies in the kind of work which is done, but simply in its having, or not having, this divine purpose. The housemaid, the peasant, the cobbler, the industrial worker have equal title to divine nobility as the judge, the abbot, the artist or the king, if they do their work as a divine "calling" or vocation. The valuation of work is shifted from the "what" to the "why" and "how".[1]

It is a little difficult to justify such a "levelling" attitude, when confronted by the real hierarchy of "vocation values" in daily life, but of this more later.

Luther "refuses to make that sharp distinction between sacred and secular so characteristic of the Latin world".[2] "The obligation to 'be perfect' rested upon every believer, in every sort of earthly calling."[3] It is easy to see how the "little monk", defying the powers of Church and State, and

[1] Brunner, *Christianity and Civilization*, II, pp. 61, 62
[2] Figgis, *From Gerson to Grotius*, p. 59.
[3] Calhoun, *op. cit.*, p. 50.

appealing to the Word of God and his own conscience, ushered in a new era in all matters of faith, conduct, and the community. It is not easy to see how the great achievements of modern industrialism could have been gained by men accustomed to make use of the confessional, not because the habit of confession would have checked the abuses of modern industry, but because it was the sturdy self-reliance bred and encouraged by the Protestant type of faith and character that made both the achievements and the abuses possible. To this day the Roman Church and the countries it dominated have stood aloof from, and been somewhat suspicious of, the strenuous industrial activities of the more progressive and therefore more prosperous Protestant countries. This is no accident, nor is it to be explained by the absence of mineral resources, or considerations of climate and national characteristics. The command of man over nature, in science and industry, has been largely due to the new emphasis thrown by the Reformers upon the practical and "secular" alongside the contemplative and "sacred" aspects of the spiritual life.[1]

A further distinction has to be drawn. Luther, especially after the outbreak of the Peasants' War, became socially and economically more and more conservative. Like Calvin and Melancthon he disliked commerce intensely, and he tried to make the social changes he was forced to sanction as little revolutionary as possible. He was also desperately afraid of any conception which might revive ideas of "merit" to the detriment of "justification by faith" alone. So the Lutheran interpretation of 1 Corinthians 7 was quietistic, even reactionary, emphasizing the duty of passive obedience, the negative side of vocation rather than the positive, abiding in one's calling rather than exerting oneself in it. Troeltsch has made a special study of the reasons for the "social

[1] Cf. Fanfani: "These facts (of Protestant thrift and enterprise) are perfectly true, but are in no way connected with the religion of the social groups concerned" (*op. cit.*, p. 186). See also p. 210, "the main explanation must lie with circumstances extraneous to the religious phenomenon".

impotence of Lutheranism".[1] It is only fair to point out that Lutherans in general refuse to accept Troeltsch's verdict on Luther and Lutheranism. Pastor Niemoeller and Bishop Bergyrav are no quietists. But the weakness Troeltsch points out may still be partly responsible for the domination of *Realpolitik* in Germany,[2] with its strong leanings towards medievalism, and the radical "active character of Calvinism . . . its capacity to penetrate the political and economic movements of Western nations with its religious ideal, a capacity which Lutheranism lacked from the very beginning".[3] For better or for worse, the Calvinist emphasis upon predestination has sent men out into their daily work with the sense of being the agents of Omnipotence, to make trial of their election by stern devotion to duty. Success in a man's secular vocation is too often wrongly considered as a confirmation of his election. Too often, also, prosperity and wealth have been treated as an index of a man's true worth or a nation's standing in the sight of God. Calvinism did not hold aloof from affairs as Romanism and even Lutheranism did, but accepted "business" as the appointed sphere for the testing and strengthening of souls. Ambition was consecrated by obtaining a religious sanction, and became a worthy motive by being sublimated into a sense of vocation, and many of the best and some of the worst things of our modern life are the result. For sometimes the "sublimation" has been little better than a disguise. ("Its sanctification of secular tasks led inevitably to a sanctification of secular motives which it did not desire but could not prevent.")[4]

Troeltsch and Tawney developed Weber's thesis, tracing the influence of the sense of vocation through the later developments of Protestantism and the rise of capitalism. In

[1] *The Social Teaching*, II, p. 563.
[2] See Figgis, *From Gerson to Grotius*, Lecture III, for the unholy alliance between Lutheranism and Machiavellianism.
[3] *The Social Teaching*, II, p. 577. "It was Calvin who finally destroyed the last vestiges of medievalism by justifying interest" (Reinhold Niebuhr, *Does Civilization Need Religion?*, p. 94).
[4] Reinhold Niebuhr, *op. cit.*, p. 102.

157

particular, they have emphasized the way in which Puritanism has been largely responsible for industrial development, for it has sent men wholeheartedly into affairs with an ascetic assiduity and concentration, and made them "religious in it", spare-living, hard-thinking, straight-dealing, giving "the more diligence to make their calling and election sure" (2 Peter 1: 10). The facts are indisputable, but both writers claim they can also observe a change in the character of Calvinism, as its close relationship with the world of business reacted upon its own spiritual life, very much as after Constantine the relationship with the State transformed and "naturalized" the Church.[1] Troeltsch especially draws attention to the difference between the attitude of Calvin himself and early Calvinism, and the later attitude of neo-Calvinism to business life.[2] Calhoun blames the Reformation for having "no coherent and realistic insight into the connection between ethical ideals and economic facts".[3] Further, while the revolt against indulgences was a symptom of a new ethical attitude, which dealt with the whole individual as the moral unit, and refused to treat his separate actions as isolated assessable moral atoms, the moral gain in this was counterbalanced by the excessive individualism of the new teaching, in both faith and conscience. (The sale of indulgences was itself a dreadful form of capitalistic exploitation!) "In Protestant theory the central concept of predestination, the direct, secret, arbitrary calling by God of the elect, one by one, leads to an anti-organic conception of the individual's relation to society. . . . In strict theory work in one's earthly vocation is not primarily for the sake of contributing to the common life . . . (it) is primarily a way of expressing obedience to God, and secondarily of discovering to oneself and to others evidences of God's favour—that is, of one's enrollment among the elect—according as one's diligence issues

---

[1] But Fanfani maintains this development was normal and inevitable, the logical outcome of Protestantism, not a perversion of it (*op. cit.*, p. 199).
[2] *The Social Teaching*, II, p. 576 f.
[3] *Op. cit.*, p. 49.

in prosperous and tranquil life."[1] While we must not exaggerate either the supposed unity of Church and State in the Middle Ages, or the supposed divisive sectarianism of Protestantism, we must admit that certain of the individualistic tendencies of our modern social and economic life gain at least the colour of an excuse from the severe loneliness of the soul with God which was at once the strength and the weakness of Protestantism, in spite of the emphasis laid by the Reformers on the Church.

But it is quite another thing to jump to the conclusion that capitalism with all its vices is the acknowledged and only legitimate child of the Reformation. "The Reformers read their Old Testament, and, trying to imitate the Jews, became those detestable Puritans to whom we owe, not merely Grundyism and Podsnappery, but also (as Weber and Tawney have shown) all that was and still is vilest, cruellest, most anti-human in the modern capitalist system."[2] It is hard to find a statement where prejudice leads to a conclusion more unwarrantable. Yet it may lead us to an important distinction too often neglected, namely, that between *industrialism* and *capitalism*. Max Weber points out that "the *auri sacra fames* is as old as the history of man",[3] but though the "spirit of capitalism" was present in germ, it could not develop until the industrial age brought into being a *system* to embody and promote that *spirit*.[4] So, too, H. M. Robertson: "We have lived in an acquisitive society for some thousands of years."[5] Aristotle deals with it in Book I of the *Politics*, and Robertson, following Sombart, and Tawney in Chapter I of *Religion and the Rise of Capitalism*, have shown how prevalent the "spirit of capitalism" was before the Reformation, and how the Church fought in vain to restrain

[1] Calhoun, *op. cit.*, pp. 46-47; cf. Fanfani, *op. cit.*, p. 149, for the Roman view.
[2] Aldous Huxley (quoted in H. M. Robertson, *The Rise of Economic Individualism*, p. 208).
[3] *The Protestant Ethic*, p. 57.
[4] Capitalism, according to Lemoine, "does not exist till it constitutes an 'entire régime' ". Quoted by Fanfani, *op. cit.*, p. 19.
[5] *Op. cit.*, p. 35.

avarice and regulate "usury". Brodrick in his brilliant piece of polemic, *The Economic Morals of the Jesuits*, left Robertson's central thesis unassailed, because it is true and unassailable. The rise of the "capitalistic spirit" can be traced back far before the Reformation, and first the Roman Church and afterwards both Romans and Protestants tried in vain to curb it, and to discover ethical principles which would apply to the rapidly developing commercial and industrial life of the new age. Fanfani devotes much time to disproving the responsibility of Catholicism for the development of capitalism. He makes a subtle and acute distinction between the influence of religion as a *doctrinal system* and its influence as an *organization* on life in general and economic life in particular. But he altogether fails to observe how this distinction has as its counterpart the corresponding one on the other side between *capitalism* and *industrialism*. "The relations between capitalism and the Catholic religion must not be confused with the relations between capitalism and the Catholic Church as an organization."[1] His fifth chapter is a defence against the charge (made by Sombart, Robertson, and others) that "Catholic ethics have contributed to the formation of the bourgeois mentality".[2] But what interests us more is the inability of Catholicism to influence, promote, restrain, or give moral guidance to industrialism as an inevitable economic tendency, and Fanfani does not give us much help on this. When he says that the ethic of Catholicism is anti-capitalistic, does he mean anti-industrial? or would he go so far as to admit that Catholicism in attempting to restrain *capitalism* in the ethical interest has discouraged *industrialism* in all its forms? "The principles on which medieval Catholicism based its antipathy to commerce have been in part maintained, in part abandoned."[3] The great commercial house of the Fuggers paid 54 per cent for sixteen years before the death of its head, a Count of the Empire, and a good

[1] *Op. cit.* p. 3. [2] *Op. cit.*, p. 149. [3] *Op. cit.*, p. 133.

Catholic.[1] The early Reformers were at first no more favourable to "usury" than the Catholics were. Robertson has shown the desperate expedients of those who relied on the confessional to give guidance and prevent abuses, and their failure to deal with the new situation. It was no longer possible to determine the "just price" from either confessional or pulpit. Tawney has described the struggle and failure of the Protestant divines to legislate for the new circumstances and problems, till Baxter's *Directory* practically marks the end of Protestant casuistry, in this country at any rate.[2] "Capitalism" was not produced either by Catholicism or by Protestantism. Both tried to suppress its earlier phases, and both failed. But Protestantism could not withdraw from the conflict, as Romanism did, for Protestantism made modern *industrialism* possible, while Romanism did not. It is a complete mistake to maintain that Protestantism *produced* capitalism, changed the sin of avarice into the virtue of consecrated industry, and then failed to control or discipline the tremendous and ruthless power it had itself produced, till that power became to a huge extent anti-social and anti-religious, and the legacy of the "detestable Puritans" has ruined us all, like the water released by the sorcerer's apprentice. *Capitalism* is much older even than the Pharaohs, it is as old as selfishness, which is as old as sin. Its growth in the modern age is mainly due to economic factors for which religion in no form is directly or indirectly responsible. Is anyone prepared to condemn *industrialism*, root and branch, the whole process by which men have advanced from a kind of life which was "poor, nasty, brutish, and short", to a stage of culture and civilization in which the standard of decency and humanity has been raised so much higher, man's power over nature has been achieved, and the possibilities of life, moral as well as material, have been indefinitely extended? Are we prepared to condemn nationalism and all its

[1] Tawney, *op. cit.*, p. 79, a most devastating passage.
[2] But see *The New Whole Duty of Man*, in numerous editions.

works, because of its abuse by unscrupulous would-be Caesars? Or to sweep away the whole of modern science, because it has produced poison gas and atom bombs? *Industrialism* is one thing, and *capitalism* far from being the same thing. But we need not even condemn capitalism unheard, as being in essence and actuality mere embodied avarice. "It is noteworthy", says Robertson, "that the writings of the religio-sociological school on the origins of the capitalist spirit are infected with a deep hatred of capitalism."[1] If capitalism is "a Moloch of Calvinist selfishness", then Weber and Tawney are the allies of Marx in their attack on capitalism; and incidentally all three lend colour to the suspicion that Protestantism after all is the root evil of our modern age, and capitalism only the inevitable nemesis of the Reformation. Indeed, to some it has become a modern substitute for the devil, as a demonic power responsible for all evil. We might with almost equal justification maintain that because Aristotle was the tutor of Alexander, he was responsible for his pupil's megalomania; and because Seneca was the tutor of Nero, Stoicism was responsible for the burning of Rome; and generalizing, a philosophic upbringing leads in later life to an ungovernable temper!

Many factors were responsible for the rise of industrialism, and for its excessive individualism, and among them were some purely economic, and apparently inevitable; but also there is no doubt that the spirit of integrity and diligence, typical of those who believed their conduct in business a matter of moment to God, created the credit and the enterprise necessary for modern business ventures. There is nothing to be ashamed of in this. That these often degenerated into exploitation and speculation is no fault of religion, but of human nature and original sin. In this sense both capitalism and nationalism are by-products of the Reformation, but we have no real cause to be ashamed of the relationship between Protestantism and the great developments of the

[1] Tawney, *op. cit.*, p. 207.

last four hundred years in politics, in industry, in science and philosophy. Admittedly in all these spheres unforeseen evils have arisen, and problems still exist which meantime defy solution, some of them due to the Renaissance more than to the Reformation; for the modern age has not yet learned to reconcile these two great formative influences. Meantime, Luther and Calvin are blamed for sins that should be laid at the door of Machiavelli and humanism in general. If there had been no Reformation many of these problems *might* never have arisen, as a ship that lies in harbour cannot run upon the rocks. As Fanfani sees clearly, it is the assertion of the moral autonomy of the individual conscience, due to the Reformation, that is responsible for much that is worst in our modern social life. But it is also responsible for the best. Even the present ills of society will surely not persuade us to renounce that autonomy, to which we owe the greatest achievements, political, economic, scientific, and religious, of the Reformation era, and to attempt to "arrest the trend towards autonomy of morals".[1] But it is possible to argue, and in fact to bring a great deal of evidence in support of the contention, that when we abandon Luther's double appeal to conscience *and* to the Word of God, we must get the false individualism that is so dangerous. Conscience emancipated from, indifferent to, or ignorant of the Word of God is no reliable guide for individual behaviour or social integration.

"Catholicism cannot recognize certain liberties in the absence of which capitalism becomes transformed or dies."[2] So Fanfani maintains it is equally opposed to parliamentary government, which is the political counterpart of capitalism, and to communism, which he treats as merely the climax of capitalism. It is quite true that the same qualities of character that made Protestantism take the lead in industrial and commercial development have made the Protestant countries the pioneers also in constitutional government. Here, again, we can admit a close relationship between Protestantism,

[1] *Op. cit.*, p. 144.   [2] *Ibid.*, p. 142.

industrialism, and political democracy, without being obliged to admit that either Protestantism or democracy stands or falls with *capitalism* in its present form.

We need not admit the Marxist contention, which the Romanist sometimes supports, that parliamentary democracy is a mere ideological façade for capitalism, which disguises its inherent exploitation. The roots of democracy are deeper than this and in purer soil. It is interesting to note how the democracies based on the French Revolution are crumbling, while those based on the Reformation still show signs of vitality. The doctrines of the sovereignty of God and of the spiritual priesthood of all believers are vital principles, fundamental to true democracy.

It is the conflict between political democracy and industrial autocracy in the Western world that is leading certain countries towards the development of democracy in industry, and certain others towards autocracy in politics. Fanfani maintains that the rise of capitalism was due in the first instance to a waning of faith (in the Catholic sense);[1] that capitalism was responsible for the creation of parliamentary government, as the best political means of furthering commercial enterprise; and now the decay of liberalism in the broad political sense is one symptom of the passing of the capitalistic era, whose political institutions reflect the economic needs and aims that create them. Apparently he regards the corporative state as the means by which the "capitalistic spirit" is to be exorcised, industrialism ethicized, and the divisive tendencies of political democracy to be transcended in a type of community where authority imposes a social conception of wealth in the interests of "the supernatural ends of the individual", and "arrests the trend towards autonomy of morals", which is to him the characteristic of the Protestant capitalistic era.[2]

[1] *Op. cit.*, p. 178.
[2] Of course, Fanfani was writing before either Mussolini or Hitler had assumed "demonic" dimensions. On this whole issue see Demant, "Religion and the Decline of Capitalism", *The Listener*, May 11–July 6, 1950.

Even those who are prepared to contemplate the passing of *capitalism* with comparative equanimity may well be alarmed at the prospect that it may carry with it the political institutions in which, in this country at any rate, our ideals of liberty, justice, and progress are more or less adequately embodied. But here again our distinction between *industrialism* and *capitalism* shows us the fallacy involved. Our political institutions *are* those of an industrialized civilization, influenced by its present phase of *capitalism*, but capable of adjustment as the economic needs and tendencies of the times may require, and also capable of directing those tendencies towards desirable social ends and restraining them from anti-social expressions. Unless we blindly accept Marxist economic determinism, we are bound by a dispassionate observation of history to admit both the moulding of our political and ecclesiastical institutions by economic pressures, and the equally obvious moulding of these economic tendencies by political and religious ideals and motives.

We may quote two recent estimates of the Weber thesis, the first by neo-Thomists and the second by a Protestant. Borne and Henry say:

> First. It is certainly impossible to establish a definite and rigorous identity between Calvinism and the spirit of capitalism, for the simple reason, in the first place, that the capitalist spirit existed long before the Reformation, as for example in numerous Italian communities of the fourteenth and fifteenth centuries.
>
> Second. In spite of the somewhat close correspondence which exists between certain Calvinistic views and the new forms of economic morality, the new spirit did not necessarily develop in all Calvinistic societies (just as A. E. Sayons believes he is able to prove that it is scarcely in evidence in Geneva itself).
>
> Third. Even when the coincidence exists between a society of Calvinistic inspiration and a new economic attitude, many other causes in the social and political spheres can exercise their influences.

All these reservations explain the justifiable mistrust felt and expressed by pure historians towards generalizations which are too rapidly drawn: and for this reason Tawney and then Robertson have severely criticized the ideas of Max Weber. But it seems that the problem has not always been clearly enunciated.

It would certainly be a serious historical error, if the object were to allege that in all cases Calvinism has been the main cause of the development of the capitalistic spirit.

In reality, it is less a question of defining a relationship of cause and effect, one sided and exclusive, than of establishing correspondences. There are times when the evolution of ideas and of the forms of economic life offer to the eyes a certain parallelism, and other moments when, on the contrary, one sees divergences and collisions. The concordance appears sometimes to manifest itself in a very acute fashion in the problem in which we are now concerned, between a religious mentality and an economic attitude. Such is the nature of the question which no doubt calls for new studies and efforts at accuracy. It seems impossible to elude the question.[1]

Compare this with Brunner: "The tiny bit of truth lying in Weber's thesis is almost irrelevant compared with the ... great injustice which it has done to Calvinist faith."[2]

Vocation is the "sublimation" of that instinctive and ineradicable *conatus in suo esse perseverare*, which, lacking sublimation, becomes perverted into ambition. Calvinism has been the only type of the Christian religion to attempt to apply this principle thoroughly and constructively to men's daily life. It has not been wholly successful either socially or with the individual. "The radical sects did challenge the existing structure of society, but their strategy in dealing with it was usually based either on apocalypticism or asceticism. The Quakers were an exception. It remained for Calvinism to develop a world-changing ethic and then to put its stamp of approval on the new world structure which came with modern capitalism. In effect *Calvinism allowed its own ethic to crystallize around the institutions of capitalism very much*

[1] *A Philosophy of Work*, p. 59n.
[2] *Christianity and Civilization*, II, p. 100.

as the ethic of the medieval church was crystallized around the insti-tutions of feudalism."[1] It would have been strange if the vary ing fortunes of four hundred years had not revealed some imperfections in the beliefs and plans of the Reformers, and produced some new aberrations as well. Neither the Church nor the State is yet organized as a "cosmos of callings" as that ideal is set before us in Eph. 4. As Troeltsch in particular has shown, Calvin is one thing and Calvinism another thing; and as for capitalism, its form to-day is very different from that of ten, twenty, or thirty years ago.[2] Far from Protes-tantism being doomed to pass with the transformation of capitalism into something new and strange, it is itself one of the strongest influences making for that transformation into something with more resemblance to the Kingdom of God.

[1] J. C. Bennett, *Social Salvation*, p. 106 (italics mine).

[2] See De Man, *Joy in Work*, for a fascinating description of the possibilities of "a greatly improved Athens with machines as slaves" (p. 143) when men succeed in using the new techniques for the highest ethical ends. It may not be a bad thing if the aims of thought and of life are not the same as the direct aims of work, if this means that the material aspects of work, its production, profit and pay, no longer fill the whole horizon. *Industrialism* is the means by which civilized man has secured emancipation from the drudgery involved in primitive man's struggle to survive. If all man's energies of body and mind are no longer required to enable him to live he may have greater opportunity to live well in the ethical sense. He may recover "the lost world of cheerful labour" (Karl Bücher) by recognising and attending to other things besides work involved in man's chief end.

Chapter Fourteen

THE CRISIS IN "WORK" TO-DAY WITHOUT A SENSE
OF VOCATION

WE have seen that the philosophy of work is insepar-
ably bound up with our whole philosophy of life.
Without accepting the Weber thesis as gospel, we owe this
much to it, that it has drawn our attention to the close relationship between religion and economic activity; and as
against Marxism has shown that religion is, or may be, a
powerful energizing force in economic affairs, instead of
merely the camouflage of exploitation and the deification of
the *status quo*, as Marxism would try to make it out to be.

Further, when confronted by Marxism, we must recognize
if we are wise, that there is some truth in the Roman Catholic
contention that Marxism is the inevitable outcome of processes let loose at the Reformation. But the tendencies themselves did not arise out of the Reformation, but out of the
Renaissance, though the Reformation gave those Renaissance tendencies an opportunity to secure their own autonomy, which they never would have had if they had not
escaped from clerical, medieval domination.[1] A materialist
will claim that it was gunpowder and printing between them
which destroyed feudalism, and it is well to recognize all the
factors involved, or at least the most important of them,
material as well as spiritual. In fact, it was the convergence

[1] See Reinhold Niebuhr, *The Nature and Destiny of Man*, Vol. I, Chap. III;
Vol. II, Chaps. VI, VII and VIII.

of material and spiritual factors that ushered in the new Renaissance-Reformation era. The materialist and the abstract idealist each see only half the picture, and neither can understand the part he sees for lack of the other.

It is when such spiritual and material factors coincide or converge that a new age can be born. So it was four hundred years ago, and all indications are that it is so to-day, when in this age of steam, petrol, electricity and atomic energy, we are living in a few years through changes that before would have occupied aeons of history. These aeons are now jostling one another as they hasten across the stage of contemporary history, and we are left breathless, actors and spectators alike. Both space and time have turned into revolutionary agents, till the word crisis has now lost all its meaning.

In a sense Machiavelli and Luther were unconscious allies in ushering in the new age. And a feature of that new age was that many provinces of human interest, formerly dominated by the Church, threw off *clerical* control and too often imagined that their new-found secular autonomy secured them also emancipation from the sway of *moral* principles. They thought they could now make their own rules as self-sufficient, self-contained spheres of human activity, governed solely by their own technical rules. We see this in "Art for art's sake", "My country right or wrong", "Business is business", and many similar epigrams, which express the claims to autonomy of the "lost provinces of religion". Painting rebelled against the endless Holy Families, and began to try to paint human life in its natural colours, a process which may now have reached its nemesis when art is so entirely divorced from religion that it can no longer even depict the human form without grotesque distortion. In international affairs pure expediency was supposed to be the only law, and in economic affairs men found themselves no longer bound to a "just price" or fair rate of interest determined by the Church, and imagined that the laws of supply and demand operating automatically would secure social justice and economic equilibrium. We have outgrown that belief. "The Economic Man" is dead, "unhousel'd, disappointed, unanel'd". The modern politician steps in where the medieval priest has ceased to tread and tries to regulate prices and control markets in the common interest. The modern world has secured political freedom, but in this liberty the individual has lost all sense of security and our free societies are haunted by the twin spectres of unemployment and war. The most dangerous feature of our time is the "Angst", or anxiety, that besets both individuals and their societies. The "work-frenzy" of which Brunner speaks is one consequence of this "Angst".

If men have to choose between liberty and security they will almost invariably choose security. If they have to choose between political liberty or economic security, which means food, there is equally little doubt what they will choose. Atomized individuals in a disintegrating society will plunge into any form of social solidarity that gives them the feeling of belonging and offers some sense of significance and purpose to their work and their lives. They will cheerfully abandon both the political liberty that they find intolerable because of its loneliness and insecurity, and the material advantages of pay or profit or comfort that may be all that a liberal democratic regime can offer them. This is the explanation of the "catholicism of despair" into which some of the more sensitive spirits of our age throw themselves, and also of the appeal of fascist and communist systems. All three totalitarian systems claim to provide absolutes and a spiritual home where man's soul can "belong". An age in which elementary spiritual needs and artificial economic pressures conspire to compel men to "go collective", needs the real fellowship of faith in the Church as never before.

Important questions arise as soon as we see that the economic sphere is not a self-contained unity, governed by its own laws, but, as a branch of human activity, it must further spiritual purposes and obey moral laws. What then are those spiritual purposes and what are those moral laws? and how can they be applied as "middle principles" to this intractable sphere of economic activity which undoubtedly has its own technical rules, and which left to itself will make its own limited aims into absolutes, and so create a new work-idolatry.

Professor Demant's masterly analysis, in his broadcast lectures on "Religion and the Decline of Capitalism",[1] deserves close study and must command general approval, especially in the stress he lays on the recent tendency, not merely to claim complete autonomy for the economic sphere from clerical control and ethical standards, but to construe the whole of life in economic terms and judge it by the standards of the market-place. Hence arises what he calls the "eccentricity" both of "economic man" and of the attempts to counteract the selfishness of economic man by collective action in the same dimension.

Hitler, Mussolini, Stalin and Franklin Roosevelt have all taught us something, and the necessities of the time have taught us more, and even more bitter lessons. *The economic situation of man can be manipulated though not endlessly, by governments and individuals.* Economic "laws" are not absolutes. In America Trusts and anti-Trust laws interfered with *laissez-faire* liberty, and in Britain war-time controls followed by nationalization have transformed economic systems. *Laissez-faire* liberty is intolerable in a shrinking world of atomized individuals with resources of food, oil, coal and whatnot so miserably inadequate for more than a few years' use in our wasteful ways of treating them, and various forms of artificial control are increasingly inevitable. Again the question arises who has the right to control? and why? and how? On the purely economic level there are no answers, or perhaps too many answers; but the moment we ask the question we begin to see how this problem of work becomes insoluble without religion. It is inevitable that a movement like com-

[1] *The Listener*, May 11–July 6, 1950.

munism will sweep from country to country, and capture workers and intelligentsia alike, if the only philosophy of life men have in the so-called pluto-democracies is "work for work's sake" or "work for the sake of profit", or merely for the sake of production, assessed in material terms.

The Reformation went a long way to transform the Church into a classless society, where *a priori* privilege gave way to the priesthood of all believers. Now communism attempts to apply the same procedure to society at large without religion. It can succeed only if it can so transform human nature that brotherhood alone provides an adequate incentive to citizenship. The lesson of history surely is that only grace can do this. It is not a secular possibility. The materialist revolutionary thinks he can usher in Utopia by turning all the ivory towers into service-stations, the idealist tries to transform business life into public service by enshrining a replica of the Grail in a glass case in the Stock Exchange. As Christian believers, we are more realistic in our approach to all these problems. We have no concern with Utopia, we are under no delusions about human nature, we keep our eyes open to the stern necessities of life, and yet we hold the clue to moral and social possibilities, of vision and of power, revealed and made available in Christ, that without Him are mere dreams and even delusions.

The Marxist Revolution in a sense may be said to be endeavouring to repeat the Reformation process, when the monk was deposed from his ethical supremacy and the good householder put in his place. The man who accepted his place in life, his station and its duties as the direct will and purpose of God for his life, and served God with diligence and devotion in that walk of life into which it had pleased God to lead him—he was the symbol and type of the religious man. But, says the Marxist, borrowing now from Weber (and others), this conscientious responsible householder has now degenerated into "the man of property", and his sense of consecration and devotion to duty as in the sight of God are now mere avarice and exploitation. He uses his religion, or the religion of his forefathers, as a disguise for his ruthless disregard of the rights of his fellows. He may or may not have retained the religion of his fathers, but in any case it is, or was, "bourgeois" ideology, a kind of smoke-screen of "free enterprise" to hide industrial maladjustments and social injustice. We must admit that the sons of the Manse do tend to become heads of departments, the grandson of the Puritan may become an unscrupulous "go-getter", if the Puritan did not have in his own life and his home the rhythm of work and joy, and in his worship penitence, which is the true source of joy and of spiritual power in any real sense.

Marxist dialectic materialism is "realistic" and maintains that capitalist democratic bourgeois thinking is "idealistic" and therefore illusory. It holds the whole bourgeois order of values is a perverted one; it is the Aristotelian, Greek, aristocratic hierarchy of values over again, with money now exalted into the vacant place of God.[1] It has reversed the natural order of means and ends. Now one must begin from the fact and importance of toil, and the whole social structure is shown to rest on and be built up from the foundation of the plain man's labour. To the Greek, leisure, culture, and the whole life of the spirit (and of the citizen) depended on the drudgery of the disfranchised helot and slave. To the medieval thinker, the culture of palace and monastery depended on the drudgery of the serf.[2] Luther overturned the monk in favour of the householder. Marx overturns the householder in favour of the labourer—the proletarian, the producer. No longer is culture to be based upon exploitation. Now the "idealistic" order, in which spiritual culture ruled over economic drudgery, is to be replaced by a realistic (materialistic) order in which the producer, despised by Greeks, by feudal prince and bourgeois economist, is now to

[1] See Brunner, *Christianity and Civilization*, II, pp. 58 ff.
[2] "Liberty in the Middle Ages depended on property, and as the serf had no property, he had no liberty; when monasticism was at its height half the population was in bondage."—Lord Acton.

come into his own, and to create a culture thrown up by the toiling masses.[1] No longer will a cultural *élite* dictate to the masses of producers. "I do not hesitate to give a large measure of credit to this Marxian 'debunking' of a false, dualistic conception of work. By this Marxian reaction the worker—now the labourer—becomes the 'real man'. The one who, according to the Aristotelian and the medieval theories was the lowest, the producer of economic values, now becomes the true bearer of human history and civilization. The working man is the hero of the social revolution and its eschatology. He is the centre of the new myth and the content of the new religion."[2]

But unfortunately for the Communist a materialistic philosophy of life cannot build work into an integral part of a social structure, where each member and organ has significance because it contributes to a whole which has real spiritual importance and purpose. Communism tried to eliminate the profit-motive and soon found that the bare idea of service of the cause could not continue to keep enthusiasm at fever pitch. Even when profits were supposed to be eliminated, the problem of the sufficient incentive took its place. All indications point to the fact that the ethical vacuum has been filled by the seven devils of the power-motive, with results that Lord Acton enables us to foretell. In the last war Communism in Russia swung over into extreme nationalism and also postponed the principle of "from each according to his capacity, to each according to his need", to exploit Stakhanovist and other methods of boosting production. Indeed it is probable that Sovietism can only maintain itself by exciting a war psychology.[3] Instead of the Marxist society developing in an equalitarian direction, we see a new hierarchy of privilege being created, and indeed there are signs of attempts to create a new industrial heroism.

[1] See Brunner, *op. cit.*, Chap. V. *passim*, and the Lysenko controversy.
[2] Brunner, *op. cit.*, p. 60.
[3] See p. 70.

"Enthusiasm is work: work is enthusiasm."[1] "The Russian Social Federated Republic declares labour the duty of all citizens of the republic."[2] Work is not an end in itself but a means to some end, not mere production for production's sake, but for some common good not itself assessable in material terms. The Communist ethic cannot treat man (the individual soul) as an end in himself without sacrificing the supreme and absolute authority of the State. On Marxist theory the State should wither away with the establishment of a classless society, but in Soviet practice the State has become as much the be-all and end-all as in Fascism.[3] It is probable that only on the religious assessment of the individual does he become an end in himself. The immortality of the soul is the postulate of civil liberty. Sovietism has not escaped from or discovered the antidote to the corrupting influences of industrialism. More and more it becomes apparent that a secular society is a contradiction in set terms, because it can only maintain itself by deifying the State.

"Contrary to the plans of Divine Providence, the work of man has, under these conditions, a tendency to become an instrument of depravement; inert matter, it is true, comes from the factory or workshop with a nobility added to it, whilst men emerge therefrom in a state of degradation."[4] Communism shows no sign of having overcome this tendency of industrialism. If it be true that religion has something vital to contribute to man's work and vice versa, a godless, secular type of society cannot make and receive that reciprocal contribution, and not even when its cause is erected into a pseudo-religion can we get a view much, if any, better than the work-fanaticism that besets degenerate capitalism. "A regime which demands heroism to make it

[1] Stalin. Quoted by Borne and Henry, *op. cit.*, p. 188.
[2] *Constitution of U.S.S.R.*, 1924.
[3] "Stalin a year or two ago announced that the party no longer holds that the State will wither away." (Demant, *The Listener*, June 1, 1950, p. 956.)
[4] Papal Encyclical, *Quadragesimo Anno*.

bearable makes open confession of its inhumanity."[1] Twelve to fifteen million slave labourers toil and die to maintain the Soviet economy and would envy the Greek helot and slave their privileges and immunities.[2] It is no accident that Russia has always refused to join the I.L.O. We must not pretend that the failures of Soviet administration necessarily disprove Marxist principles, any more than the failures of the Church detract from the message of salvation in the Gospel. Most of the East to-day is looking towards Soviet Russia because they believe thay have nothing to hope for from the West, but commercial exploitation. But it is a fair criticism, made by Brunner,[3] that historical dialectical materialism in its "transvaluation of values from the spiritual to the material, economic scale of values" is "only a last phase of bourgeois capitalism". "The dispute between Marx and the capitalists is much concerned with who should have money; it being admitted tacitly by both parties that money rules the world."[4] Marxism has its Utopian dream too, but it too often and too easily treats economic pressures as the sole powers and economic goods as the sole values in life, and so fails altogether to get a coherent view of work where spiritual ideals and economic interests are both recognized, but not on terms of equality, for economic interests must be made relative and instrumental to truly spiritual ideals and purposes.

"Vocation is at once the standard by which the validity of industry is to be tested and an incentive by which it will be most effectively carried on. It is the starting-point for the Christian in approaching the problem of motive in industry."[5]

We seem to have in Soviet practice a far worse perversion of the sense of vocation than the theme of the Weber thesis. A sense of vocation—"mission"—is necessary for the continued well-being of the community, but on a basis of materialism such a sense of vocation would be merely a claim

[1] Borne and Henry, *op. cit.*, p. 189.   [2] See new Report to U.N.
[3] *Op. cit.*, p. 60.   [4] *Ibid.*   [5] Reckitt, *Faith and Society*, p. 341.

176

to be a man of destiny without the sense of responsibility that might save such a claim from becoming demonic. *Such sense of vocation as we can have on materialist terms must become devastating and demonic.* Anyone who has ever had anything to do with unemployed men knows how enforced idleness saps a man's moral stamina, makes him lose his social status, his self-respect and ultimately doubt of his own salvation; so intimately are the three senses of vocation bound up together, that when he can no longer express himself in satisfying and socially useful work, he will lose all sense of significance and purpose in his life, and therefore cease to believe God cares for him. The same thing also affects those who have turned their work into an idolatry, their values all become perverted, and instead of working to live they live to work. But it is not altogether true that we work to live, merely in the sense that we work only to earn our daily bread, we work because work is not only necessary for the continuance of our existence, but because it is the activity (*energeia*) of man, made in the image of God, who has inherited the urge of creation from his Maker. We work in the last resort to please God. It is unlikely that the moral effect of Stakhanovitism will in the long run be any better than that of big business, and all indications are that it is far more dangerous socially and morally. *A materialistic "sense of vocation" cannot create a free and responsible society,* and it must inevitably fall victim to the terrible realities described by Lord Acton: "Power tends to corrupt and absolute power corrupts absolutely."[1]

If I may refer again to the Genesis story, work is not merely a necessity for man, it is a privilege, a token of his kinship with God. Man's capacity for work, and his ability to work, will always tend to produce differentiations in the various forms of society he sets up. A currency may be devalued overnight, and on the morrow everyone waken up to find himself poor in order that he may be induced to work hard, and so

[1] Lord Acton, *Historical Essays and Studies*, p. 504.

be forced into the labour market to make some assessable and saleable contribution. We have not seen the last New Deal. But immediately new differentiations will show themselves and a new hierarchy of privilege will be built up, in order to provide suitable incentives for all sorts of capacities. *There is nothing essentially or inevitably unethical or un-Christian about either profit or privilege, or even property for that matter.*[1] There is no reason to believe that a classless society, should such be possible, would be a better society spiritually than the present very imperfect social patterns we have woven to protect and sustain our feeble souls.

In support of this let me quote Koestler:

> The new revolutionary incentives were: collectivism to replace individual competition; voluntary discipline instead of economic and legal coercion; the consciousness of responsibility towards the community; international class-solidarity to replace chauvinism; the dignity of labour to replace dignity of birth or position; a spirit of fraternity among equals to replace the paternity of God and Leader; reform instead of retribution; persuasion instead of compulsion; in general a new spiritual climate permeated with the feelings of brotherliness, equality, solidarity—"All for one and one for all".
>
> All this sounds to-day like bitter irony. The words "utopianism", "romantics", "sentimentality", automatically present themselves, even in the minds of convinced communists. Twenty-five years of Soviet reality have turned them into unconscious cynics; and because they want to believe that Russia means Socialism they have forgotten what Socialism really means. Without the creation of new human incentives the abolition of the capitalist incentives leaves a vacuum in which the social body becomes paralysed. A society with no incentives and ethical values will, whatever its economical structure, either dissolve into chaos and anarchy, or become a dumb mass under the whip.
>
> It was not to be expected that the new spirit of 1917 would triumph without great transitional difficulties and setbacks. But the history of the Soviet Union is not one of advances alternating with retreats. The curve of development ascends

[1] "As human nature is, it is impossible to get functional differentiation without the stimulus of privilege." Brunner, *op. cit.*, II, p. 67.

during the first decade roughly until the middle 'twenties, and from then onwards shows a continuous and uninterrupted fall until, a generation after the experiment started, the new incentives have been replaced without exception and in all walks of life by the old, abandoned ones.

The war has accelerated this development and brought it to its completion. The crowning of the Orthodox Metropolitan Sergius in Moscow Cathedral and his official recognition as Patriarch of all Russians on September 12, 1943, was a symbolic act in more than one respect; it was a confession of the Soviet regime's failure to create a new human creed, new ethical values, a new faith for which to live and die. . . . .

The Russian revolution has failed in its aim to create a new type of human society in a new moral climate. The ultimate reason for its failure was the arid nineteenth-century materialism of its doctrine. It had to fall back on the old opiates because it did not recognize man's need for spiritual nourishment.[1]

Communism has failed to manufacture a synthetic substitute for the sense of vocation which can in its reality and strength come only from faith in a living God. Now we see Russia desperately exploiting fear, both internally and externally, as a substitute for the necessary loyalty and sacrifice and goodwill that come from faith alone. And work is being preached as a gospel.

Work may become a means of grace, but it never can become in itself a gospel. It we make it so, we lose all sense of proportion. After all, in the monastery, in spite of the feudalism which sustained both palace and monastery by serf labour, there was a certain synthesis between work and worship and a certain symmetry of life in consequence. With the increasing secularization of our time we have lost that synthesis and that symmetry with the loss of all sense of purpose and all standards of values.[2] "The true motive to work comes from having a place in God's plan",[3] and I would add the sense of contributing something of value to set forward that

[1] Arthur Koestler, *The Yogi and the Commissar*, pp. 194, 195 and 200.
[2] See Demant, *Religion and the Decline of Capitalism, passim.*
[3] Brunner, *op. cit.*, II, p. 70.

plan. If it be true that the instrument of power in feudal times was the sword and in modern times is money, we must remember we are still confronted with both as uncontrolled as ever they were. Our money-poisoned world has not succeeded in banishing the sword and it may be that each successive era of human history has to confront a new spectre as well as all the unexorcised spectres of the past. Hence we meet again the problem so frequent in history when the weapons of emancipation of one age become the fetters of the next, and the individual liberty claimed by the Reformers, when the sap of religion has gone out of it, becomes the exploitation of *laissez-faire*.

It may be that the function of Karl Marx is to force us to take the Reformation seriously, and *rescue Protestantism from its bourgeois entanglements*. No one can pretend that our standards of values within the Church show that we are no respecters of persons, nor is the world within which we live constructed on lines which make it easy for most men and women to treat their jobs as Christian vocations. We still hanker after the leisure and affluence of the gentleman who can live without the necessity of working, and unconsciously we treat him alone as emancipated from the curse of toil, while the manual worker is still subject to it. But the Church should not be dragged at the chariot wheel of the State, when the latter swings over from a gentleman-ethic to a producer-ethic. Over against the world, which judges everything in terms of *market values*, the Church should work out for itself standards and scales of *vocation values*. It has already done so to an imperfect extent in the case of the ministry. Not one in twenty of our ministers would be in the ministry because of an interest in market values, or professional standards, or social status, or that sort of thing, but because the cure of souls, while a dangerous *trade*, and a miserably paid *profession*, is so rich in vocation values that a man of spiritual devotion can find no such rewarding life anywhere else. In the conditions of human life joy is possible only for those who are active in worthwhile and effective employments. The joy is in the activity as well as in the achievement, and in the leisure and contemplation that follow it.

We must constantly challenge all social patterns, standards, methods and values, with the question: Do they recognize the dignity of those engaged in trade, industry or profession? And do they give them opportunity to find liberty and joy in the performance of their duty?

Apart altogether from the lack of vocation values in certain jobs and the impossibility of treating some jobs as a "calling", there is the undoubted fact that the same job may have an entirely different effect upon the character of the worker, according to the spirit in which it is done. A somewhat hackneyed story illustrates this point. A visitor to a stone-mason's yard asked one mason, who was at work with mallet and chisel on a piece of sandstone, cutting along a chalk line: "What are you doing?" "I'm cutting this stone." He went to a second, working with similar mallet and chisel and stone, and put the same question, to be answered: "I'm earning my pay." On putting the same question to a third, he was told: "Why, I'm building a cathedral." All three were working on the stonework of the cathedral, but to the first his work was mere routine drudgery, from which he could get no satisfaction; to the second the only thought was his pay-packet at the end of the week. The third alone had the vision of the work to which he was contributing. Ruskin would say that inevitably the spirit in which the work was done would show itself in the quality of the work, and, other things being equal, he was probably right. But in any case there can be no dispute that the effect upon the character of the worker would be quite different. Every faithful pastor who knows his people intimately will bear witness that the vision of the Kingdom may illuminate even the most monotonous drudgery. In all our plans to transform the haphazard, purposeless bazaar of commodities and jobs into a cosmos of callings we should remember that recognition of a Supreme Plan and faithful devotion to the duties of my station, however irksome and unrewarding, with a sense of vocation, are indispensable conditions of the successful working of any economic or political programme, and of the transformation of the inevitable necessities of life into sources of spiritual opportunity.

Turn from the hackneyed illustration of the three masons to one perhaps more topical. Imagine three doctors: (1) The first is very highly skilled, has a strict sense of professional duty, but is an agnostic and scoffs at any suggestion that religion has a direct bearing upon health. Yet he will fight for every case with all the resources at his disposal. His motive is professional integrity, and it carries him a long way.

(2) The second doctor does not work so hard, nor is he so quick off the mark. He lets cases slip through his hands, is casual in his diagnosis, does not keep himself abreast of new methods of treatment, but is in his place in Church every Sunday and is a delightful person in all his family and social relationships. Religion obviously means a great deal to him.

Obviously (1) is, or will soon become, a hard man whose outlook on his patients will be to treat them as cases, interesting from a professional point of view, but not persons. And (2) equally obviously has not unified and integrated his life so that his religion leads him to improve his technical qualifications and to employ them all in his profession. His profession is one thing, his religion another.

Picture (3) a third doctor, who has so unified his faith and his profession. Take, for instance, so many of the physicians and surgeons who made the Edinburgh School of Medicine renowned all over the world. In them faith, skill and assiduity were united, so that in their profession their patients trusted them and were materially helped towards recovery by the sanctified humanity, sympathy and infectious moral power of their doctor or surgeon. I once had the opportunity of comparing the spirit and atmosphere of medicine and surgery as practised here with the corresponding spirit and atmosphere of a medical school where skill was perhaps as great as anything here, but without much real religion and, therefore, without the rich humanity of our medical practice. The money interest bulked more largely, the professional interest led doctors to concentrate on guinea-pig features of illness till patients became mere specimens of diseases and not men and women and children with souls as well as minds and bodies. Such is the difference infused into a profession by a sense of vocation.[1]

If you have ever watched by the bedside of a dying man— say in the infirmary—and noted the attitude of everyone whose duty brought them inside the screens, you will see what I mean. To some it is merely a hopeless case, now not even of clinical interest—instead of a soul on its pilgrimage. To a young probationer-nurse, it is something rather frightening; to another who has been more often in contact with death perhaps it is rather a nuisance that so many cases in her ward are dying; it offends her professional pride. But when you get the real religious sense of awe, when faith comes into the presence of the Angel of Death, even in the simplest ministrations you know the difference and so does the patient. There was a time when the Sisters took prayers in their wards on Sunday evenings in Edinburgh Royal Infirmary—the same Sisters who tended them every day—so creating a spiritual bond that was a powerful factor in promoting healing and equally powerful in consecrating even suffering and transforming it into a means of Grace.

Apply the same principle to the teaching profession, perhaps the one in most grave crisis at the present moment. Thou shalt love the Lord thy God with all thy heart and mind and soul and strength—but it takes a thorough consecration to be able to go on—and thy neighbour's children

[1] For an excellent introduction to this study of the vocational aspects of medical practice, see D. T. Jenkins, *The Doctor's Profession*.

as thyself. No profession is so intolerable as teaching unless the relation of the teacher to his pupils and to his subject be genuinely religious in quality. In no profession is a sense of vocation more necessary and the absence of it more tragic. In no profession is mere skill without dedication and the reverence of true faith—reverence for God showing itself in reverence for personality—more lamentably and incongruously inadequate. For in teaching the direct relationship of personalities is everything, and the media for that relationship, even such material ones as school-books, can be described as mere symbols of spiritual ideas and realities, and personality becomes an end in itself.

This gives us the clue to the differences in "vocation values" in the various forms of employment. That is to say, apart from or rather in addition to the all-important question of motive, giving spiritual significance to every necessary employment, there is a difference in the spiritual standing of various crafts, professions, and callings. Generally speaking, where a job involves direct personal dealings with other persons as persons, and not as mere cogs in machinery, it will tend to influence character for good, and be more spiritually satisfying than a job that merely deals with things and people as they are involved in the natural world. The doctor and the nurse, the teacher and the minister, have more spiritually rewarding vocations than the stonemason, if they treat their calling as God's will for them and seek to praise and glorify God in it. It is very difficult to get the cathedral sense into everyone contributing to the building even of the cathedral, and you would normally expect most of those so engaged to be merely "rude mechanicals", without the vision or the vocation that transforms their toil and duty with the inspiration of faith.[1] But when we come to the doctor, the

[1] M. B. Reckitt quotes (*Faith and Society*, p. 351) a mordant story of a man who for nine years had been making "C 429" without any idea of what it was or what it was meant to do. It would be interesting to trace how many workers all over the country were making some part of the structure or equipment of the *Queen Mary*, known before her launch as "534", without

nurse, the teacher, or the minister, the personal relationships are the most fundamental thing, and the material media of their professional practice are all directly contributing to the integration of personality and the concurrent building up of a free society. But here again we are confronted with the impossibility of gaining any standard of comparison between a musical composer whose media are mere symbols like the score of a symphony and the instruments of an orchestra, the last again being played by persons, and a sculptor, whose medium remains in its materiality, yet no longer crude marble, but now an expression of an idea, and even of a personality. We must return later to these "vocational" aspects of the subject.

the faintest idea of the significance of their work or the work of the multitudes who were contributing to the making and fitting out of the Cunarder. But every worker in every shipyard on Clydeside felt a personal pride in her when she was launched and even more when after completion she made a triumphal progress down to the open sea. In this connection the "industrial animism" by which, according to De Man, the industrial worker comes to personalize his tools and what he makes deserves careful study. (See De Man, *op. cit.*, pp. 26 ff.) The effect of the skilful use of complicated and powerful tools upon the character of the worker also deserves study. "The machine does not mechanize labour, but spiritualizes it." (Otto Kammerer). But this "animism" is not confined to the industrial worker. What sailor ever refers to his ship as "it"?

Chapter Fifteen

THE CALL TO THE MINISTRY IN A "COSMOS OF CALLINGS"[1]

LET us recall the statement of Koestler, quoted in the preceding chapter, that in practice Communism as in Russia has failed to supply an adequate ethical incentive to work and has had to fall back upon religion both in war and in peace, as well as upon the profit-motive in the shape of Stakhanovitism. This illustrates the inevitable failure of a secular idealism. It is an admission that the purely ethical motive of service to the community on the secular plane is not in its purity strong enough or stable enough, nor is it sufficiently highly charged with emotion, unless we add to it the over-tones of religion, and the under-tones of economic interest. Service of the community needs to be raised to a heroic level, as in war-time patriotism, and to be reinforced and embodied in a system of rewards, partly tangible and material, partly spiritual, such as profit, privilege and power. If citizenship is to become a predominant motive, strong enough to prevail over individual selfishness and social pressures, it must either be linked up with religion or itself assume the quality of a religion by deifying the State. That is why, in the previous chapter, I stated that we were rapidly discovering, and confirming the discovery, that a secular society is a contradiction in set terms. To maintain the loyalty

[1] For the phrase "cosmos of callings" see Troeltsch, *The Social Teaching*, I, p. 293. Obviously it is a quotation, but the source I have been unable to discover nor can anyone enlighten me. It looks like Aquinas.

and sacrifice required of its citizens, it is compelled either (1) to deify the State, in which case its pretensions and its citizens' devotion become demonic, with catastrophic results, some of which we have recently seen; or (2) to relate the authority of the State and its social discipline to the realities and powers of religion. But, fortunately or unfortunately, the Christian religion has never been content with the role of being social cement or supplying civilization and culture with an antiseptic to selfishness. The statesman and the educationalist to-day want the humanist and not the apocalyptic aspects of religion. Amos would not yet be welcomed at the Royal Chapel, nor would John the Baptist be happy in a public school. There are many to-day, who, confronted with the furious face of things, and realizing that even the cleverest gadgets fall far short of compassing man's salvation, try to "exploit religion without worshipping God".

This is exactly what seems to be happening in Russia, with what ultimate result we do not yet know. Orthodox religion in Russia has never been otherwise than Byzantine in its view of the relations of Church and State. The conception of a free Church in a free State is distinctively Western and post-Reformation at that. What immediately concerns us in the present phase of Soviet experiment is that a totalitarian State, even more than any other State, needs to inspire its citizens with a sense of loyalty capable of sacrifice even to the point of heroism. Indeed, it seems to require from its leaders and its people a fanatical devotion to a cause that brooks no rival loyalties. But a godless "sense of vocation" is a synthetic product, lacking the sense of absolute obligation and responsibility, which only religion can inspire, and inevitably prone to the *hubris* that is the idolatry of power. Communism needs in its leaders and its people a "sense of vocation". The only sense of vocation it can itself inspire is so perverted and ethically unstable that it must issue in imperialism and lust for great and more absolute power. *There is nothing in the whole world so dangerous as a sense of vocation without a belief in God*, it will inevitably issue in the apotheosis of egoism, as we see it in the Titanism of our day. *Hubris* was no invention of the Reformers, nor does Max Weber hold the copyright for the analysis of the degeneration of motives. Lord Acton anticipated him, the great Greek tragedians anticipated Lord Acton, and the devil holds the patent rights in this process all too common in history. It has been observed at work ever since the Book of Genesis. There will soon be material for another Weber thesis, if the Russian worker "offers his icons to Stakhanov", and the new Byzantine tyranny makes a bid for the domination of the world.

It is exactly the apocalyptic characteristics of true Christianity, obscured and dormant in an era liberal in its theology and liberal also in its political system, that shine out when Christianity is once more confronted with hostile and persecuting forces in the dark night of the soul. In this Year of Grace 1951 it is more than forty years since in Edinburgh the first World Missionary Conference took as its slogan: "The Evangelization of the World in this Generation". Christendom was a consolidated base, the Church was militantly engaged in working out from it to the few regions that still remained unevangelized (which to most people meant also uncivilized). The confidence of those days astonishes us, as we survey the ruins of Christendom, and desperately struggle to maintain our footing in lands a generation ago supposed to be permanently and definitely Christian. Instead of our missions in heathen lands being spearheads of a Christian civilization and culture that could command respect even among those who would not accept the Gospel at the heart of it, they are now faced in the East and elsewhere with the same problem as confronted the Early Church, how to insert the Gospel into the midst of an aggressively pagan culture, and how to insert the Church into an aggressively pagan society, without the support of a paramount power. Now for the first time since the heyday of Islam, the forces arrayed against Christianity have themselves assumed the dimensions of a religion. Communism is not a mere economic-political policy, or a philosophy; it is a missionary religion, with its own programme, its own apocalyptic visions, its own ethic and its own propaganda methods. It challenges Christianity at its very heart and home.

It is small wonder that the Church in our time has become intensely self-conscious and self-critical, perhaps so much so as to be incapable of acting as the agent of evangelism. Is its Gospel of redemption relevant to the need of our day? Is the Church as an institution relevant to the Gospel? If confidence was the keynote of Edinburgh 1910, penitence was the keynote of Amsterdam 1948.

What have we to say when confronted with a situation such as that in east Europe and in China? When under a totalitarian regime it becomes impossible for the Church to function in the way that has been taken for granted in the West, at least since the Reformation? When priests and pastors are classed as non-producers and denied ration-cards as for a time at least happened in Russia? Must we contemplate a reversion to a part-time ministry, in which ordained men (and women) will earn their daily bread by following some trade, and, after satisfying the State's requirements as "producers", devote the rest of their time to shepherding the little flock of loyal folk who remain faithful in spite of persecution and discouragement? Apart from open persecution an unfriendly State may make the institutional life of a Church almost impossible by manipulating the currency and perverting State-education into godless propaganda. Even more dangerous is the policy we already see employed in certain lands, where the State has taken over the property and the financial responsibilities of the Church and grants maintenance and countenance only if and so far as the Church accepts the role of the spiritual arm of the State, invoking supernatural sanctions for dubious national and international policies.

To come nearer home, we are building in this country a "welfare state" whose vast and complicated structure depends on the sense of citizenship and corporate responsibility of large numbers of people, whose industry and self-discipline maintain the social security and full employment that are the community aims of the welfare state. Such a regime makes higher and more constant moral demands of the population as a whole than previous haphazard social patterns, where hunger and fear operated more directly and immediately, if not always justly. The *laissez-faire* freedoms have had to be abandoned. A new structure of controls, inducements and privileges is being built up by a painful process of trial and error. This structure has to be maintained by incessant work. If we cannot induce men to do such work from motives of citizenship, reinforced by religious over-tones and economic under-tones, we shall be compelled to have recourse to totalitarian methods of compulsion to maintain the structure of the welfare state. We are facing in a less acute form the dilemma that forced Russia back into exploitation of nationalism and Stakhanovitism. So long as large numbers of men and women are earning more than ever before and living at a much higher standard of life, it is difficult to bring home to them that the country as a whole is well over the edge of the precipice of bankruptcy. It seems too difficult to convince them of the critical state of public finance, so long as they themselves have food to eat and money to spend. We have not yet solved the problem—how to prevent exploitation while providing adequate incentives to enterprise and continuous hard work. There is a form of moral devaluation of the currency that has hitherto escaped explicit notice. We all know that money can now buy much less in the shape of commodities, but we have not always noticed how much less it can buy in the shape of privilege and power and comfort. On the whole, this may be a good thing. The welfare state may be an improvement on a plutocracy, but we should recognize how much more difficult the problem of an adequate incentive has become, now that money is so much less important. *We may have been only too successful in discrediting the profit-motive.*

The stigma which formerly attached to poverty has now been transferred to property. The person who in 1900 would have described himself as a "gentleman"[1] is now characterized in the picturesque parliamentary language of 1951 as a "Spiv", so completely have our values and our culture been industrialized. But a "gentleman" whose leisure and independence emancipated him from the necessity of labour in 1900 may have been no true gentleman. Yet if all our ethical values are to be determined in terms of their contribution to exports or tangible manufactures in some form, our culture will soon become perverted into dollar worship. How far this materialistic worship of economic values has already gone a glance at our school, college and university curricula will show. The highest marks for individual subjects in the Civil Service examinations are now awarded to geography and engineering. This utilitarian distortion of cultural values will produce for the next generation leaders of various specialist, technical skills, who are on any real spiritual assessment merely displaced persons. It is to such spiritually rootless persons that the Church must in this generation minister and present the Gospel, but when we come to address them we may find that in any truly spiritual sense as persons they simply "are not there". There seems little in their preoccupied minds to which the Gospel can appeal.

The meaning of the "Call" to the ministry, and the importance of the ministry as a "Calling" have been partially dealt with in Part I, Chapter One. Here we are concerned with the relationship of the Church to the world of work, and of the ministry to the trades and professions into which we group the various employments. Confronted as we are

[1] "Why don't you find a job?" "Because I happen to have been born a gentleman, and intend to remain one." Martin Boyd, *Lucinda Brayford*, p. 276.

with the prospect that soon in many places of the world the institutional Church may fall under a ban, unless it conforms to the dictates of the State and *consents to become its agent of propaganda and morale*, the structure of the Church and the form of the ministry may suffer profound changes. Where, as in the Orthodox and Roman Churches the function of the priesthood is primarily to perform the liturgy, and the prophetic function of preaching is not so fundamental, it is possible to visualize a priesthood, earning its living by manual or other labour, and ministering to a congregation similarly employed on Sundays and Holy Days, and performing such other spiritual functions as remain possible. Indeed both Orthodox and Roman Churches are making experiments in such a priesthood, and the latter particularly, profiting by the experience of priests exercising their ministry while serving as conscripts in various armies, is now experimenting with a similar system in industry, so that in the event of the Church having to go underground because of a hostile State régime, the Sacraments may still be administered. Incidentally, also, largely under the inspiration of the two Encyclicals, *Rerum Novarum* (Leo XIII, 1891) and *Quadragesimo Anno* (Pius XI, 1931) and certain factors in Thomist teaching, the Roman Church has now a coherent and fairly adequate doctrine of the secular calling, and now no longer considers the monk, the nun (and the priest) as the sole recipients of a "call". This development at the present juncture is significant. It means that just when under the stress of necessity the gap between clergy and laity is being narrowed because the priest may have to earn his bread in productive industry, from the other side the Roman Church is drawing a little nearer to the principle of the spiritual priesthood of all believers. Necessity makes strange bed-fellows.

In Protestant Churches, with their much greater stress upon the preaching of the Word, and consequently upon an educated ministry with high professional standards and exacting training, the problem is much more difficult. Successive devaluations of currency, or "New Deals" in one country after another, have led to rapid and almost catastrophic degeneration in the social status and economic security of the ministry. No class in the community has suffered more heavily from the increase of taxation, without being in a position to exert social pressure to secure salary increases commensurate with rises in prices. The ministry contributes nothing directly to the export drive and its contribution to social morale can be secured without providing any added incentive.

It is scarcely accidental that the political pressures upon the Protestant Churches to prophesy smooth things to promote national morale, and the economic pressures of dwindling financial resources and loss of purchasing power in stipends, should coincide with the revival of Franciscan visions of a ministry which desires and accepts no social or professional status, and is content to live at a bare subsistence level, with the minimum of comforts, and perhaps benefiting less than any other section of the community from the social security that is the aim and basis of the Welfare State. The Franciscan ideal cannot be put into practice except on the basis of a celibate priesthood. There is no sign that the Church wants such a ministry. Indeed there are many elements within and without the Church to whom such a ministry would have no appeal. The ability, skill and wide range of interests required of the modern minister would make him stand very high in the professions. But in present tendencies it is more and more difficult to provide him with a reasonable competence to enable him to maintain his household at the lowest subsistence level. It is quite possible that in the near future it will only be possible to maintain religious ordinances, owing to the dearth of fully-qualified and trained ministers, by commissioning and training laymen to perform many of the duties at present by use and wont performed by the minister alone. In this respect it is noteworthy how among Protestants also, grim necessity is leading to a pretty drastic and conscience-stricken concern that the Church should be a "confessional" Church, but not a pastors' (clerical, sacerdotal) Church.

It is now widely recognized that pulpit and pew have fallen out of touch with one another. The one may have degenerated into mild metaphysics, while the other has sharpened into harsh economics. If any minister questions this, let him try to put across from his pulpit to an industrialized congregation the doctrine of Providence, whereas the man in the pew mostly thinks now in terms of insurance. The vague idealism of a liberal Gospel holds no message of redemption and indeed is scarcely relevant to the terrible pressures and all-pervading connivances of the ordinary man's everyday life.

It is worth while noting that in the ordained elder, whose office is a spiritual one as is that of the minister, we have the best symbol in Christendom for the kind of relationship we envisage between the Gospel and everyday life. In our Presbyterian Order the Bread and Wine, symbols of the broken Body and shed Blood of our Lord, are distributed to the congregation by the hands, often toil-scarred, of men ordained to exercise spiritual jurisdiction in the Church, yet earning their daily bread in secular callings. I venture to predict that if we in this country have to confront a totalitarian regime, the strongest and most significant contribution to the Church's witness will be made by the ordained elder, and by women. Yet which of us would claim that we make the most of this all-important element in our presbyterian polity, or indeed that its significance and possibilities are in any adequate sense realized or taken seriously? The plight of so many congregations when their minister was absent on war service should open our eyes to the extent of spiritual pauperization of our office-bearers and members. Rome and Orthodoxy have both seen the writing on the wall, and are preparing for the obvious dangers of the immediate future, while we Protestants, and especially we

Presbyterians, have demobilized the very armies that should be in training for the inevitable battles of the future. It is not so much that we should arouse and train our office-bearers and members for the support and defence of the Church; that would be a confession of defeat if we confined ourselves to the defensive. These should be the people who are making the faith real in their daily work and daily lives with a devout, heroic sense of vocation, and unless they are doing so, all our sermons are scarcely worth the salvage value of the paper they are written on.

There have always been members who are in the Church with mixed motives, just as there are ministers in the ministry. We live in a mixed society and it is possible to argue that in such a situation all our motives have some element of impurity in them, and even that an absolutely and abstractly pure motive is not possible among sinful man. "A service rendered by 'pure' agents, within conditions actually 'pure' in themselves, simply does not exist."[1] Even in the ministry some mixture of motives seems inevitable.

"Are not zeal for the glory of God, love to the Lord Jesus Christ, and a desire for the salvation of men, so far as you know your own heart, your *great* motives and *chief* inducements to enter into the office of the Holy Ministry?"[2]

It is a legitimate speculation that in the near future our congregations may become considerably larger, because life in this revolutionary epoch is insupportable by solitary individuals without some sense of "belonging" to relieve their "cosmic anxiety". At the same time there will probably be fewer ministers, as the secondary motives of economic security and social status, etc., no longer apply with the same force. Even a Church without a hierarchy can claim no immunity from ambition in its priests and pastors, though mercifully we presbyterians are saved by our "Presbyterian parity" from the worst manifestations of the lust for power.

[1] Brunner, *The Divine Imperative*, p. 199.
[2] *Ordinal and Service Book*, Church of Scotland, p. 22 (italics mine).

A disgruntled and unheeded prophet is every whit as dangerous spiritually as the frustrated ambition of a pushful priest. It is probable that in the foreseeable future, the ministry will hold out less attractions for the ambitious and no attraction at all for those who ask only for an easy life with reasonable comfort and security. It will lack the immediate incentives and high rewards of a skilled trade, and also perhaps the social status and privileges of a profession. It will secure as recruits only those so unmistakably called by God that they can find no happiness until they respond to that call. "The Lord God hath spoken, who can but prophesy?" (Amos 3: 8).

When Peter Simple and his friend O'Brien[1] were confronted with a hellfire negro-preacher, Peter Simple asks:

> "Is he a licensed preacher?"
> O'Brien: "Very little licence in his preaching, I take it; no, I suppose he has had a *call*."
> P. Simple: "A call! What do you mean?"
> O'Brien: "I mean that he wants to fill his belly. Hunger is a call of nature, Peter."

"Put me, I pray thee, into one of the priests' offices, that I may eat a piece of bread". (1 Samuel 2: 36) Even a priest must eat bread, or he will die.

The day is past, if it ever existed in Scotland, when an outsider could consider with approval that the ideal of the ministry is to maintain a "resident gentleman in every parish". Our Scots tradition, ever since the Reformation, even in the heyday of moderatism, has been to shepherd the souls in each parish by one who can deal with men and women of all sorts, conditions and classes, because he is "baptized into a sense of the condition of all men" (George Fox) by his Call to the Ministry, training, and consequent ordination. His whole education should aim at proving and developing his *charisma*—the gift of Grace which fits him for his multifarious duties. The ministry is a kind of focus,

[1] In Marryat's *Peter Simple*, (1888) p. 338

where Grace is concentrated and projected upon each particular human need through the personality of a man set apart from the preoccupations of the market-place to devote himself wholly to this mediation of Grace to meet human need. He is not and never can be the sole channel of Grace, but he exercises a double representative capacity. As the bearer of the Word of God, he preaches to the people and dispenses the Sacraments, as the representative of the people he offers prayer to God on their behalf. As pastor he ministers to the people in the name of God. "Blessings and needs meet in a man with a vocation". (W. M. Macgregor)

As the minister of the Gospel he can say: *Humani nil a me alienum puto*. His job is to show the supreme relevance of the Gospel of redemption to every human need. So W. M. Macgregor says: "Vocation brings the sense of relevance." Nothing can be more relevant to the present predicament than a Gospel of redemption on the lips and in the life of a man called to the ministry.

Though, as Protestants, we do not believe the only "Call" is to the ministry, nor that the Church is constituted by its hierarchy, we stoutly maintain that the ministry is no mere job which a man may choose for prudential or other reasons and exercise by employing his human talents with skill and carefulness. Even when they were developing the doctrine of the secular "Calling" the Reformers were emphatic in recognizing the distinctive nature of the ministry as the Calling *par excellence, the* representative office in which grace was focused upon human need in the preaching of the Word and the observance of the Sacraments. The Reformers were no sectaries and a "high" doctrine of the ministry as a Calling is bred in the bones of every true Presbyterian. As there are diversities of gifts, so there are diversities of Callings. In the ministry those "called" are withdrawn from the trafficking of the market-place in order to devote themselves wholly to the duties of their calling. Their "mission" involves this separation or special dedication, not as an inherent privilege of an Order conceived of as the sole channel of Grace and, therefore, raised above those who must "abide" in their secular Callings, but because of the same necessity that leads us to set apart churches from the buildings where we live and work, and the Sabbath from the occupations and amusements of other days. To the Protestant the sacred is that which redeems and consecrates the secular, not that which is segregated from it. This functional differentiation is a characteristic of the Church, which seeks in its institutional patterns to embody the charismatic diversity of individuals and "organs" of the Body of Christ. In the Presbyterian ordained elder we have the distinctive recognition of a Call to Church office, which does *not* involve abandonment of one's secular employment. It symbolizes in theory all three senses of vocation, the response to the Call of Election, the sense of Mission, and yet remaining in a secular Calling, therein to glorify God while at the same time ordained to bear rule in the Church.

If our belief in God as revealed by Jesus Christ is real, we must think of the world as under the providential care of the God who made it and sustains it as "the vale of soul-making", within which His children become more than His creatures, and rise to the full stature of their manhood in Jesus Christ. The world as it is is no pure and mere emanation of the plan and purpose of God. There are features of it that are due to the Fall of man, and not directly attributable to the positive will of God, though permitted by Him. There is evil in the world and sin in the hearts of men, and hence disorder in their relationships and in the structure of their societies, and injustice and suffering that need not be. Out of this disorder we believe it is God's will that order and justice should come in the affairs of men. We may accept the doctrine of "the Orders of Creation and of Redemption", as this has been developed especially by German writers, or we may not,[1] but we cannot deny, on any reading of the

[1] See Brunner, *Das Gebot und die Ordnungen* (English trans. *The Divine Imperative*).

Scriptures, that the world is meant to offer to men of different capacities an ordered Cosmos of Callings, in which each and all may find their fulfilment as personalities in contributing to a common good. Providence is concerned not merely with the narrowly spiritual care of souls, but with the relation of men's souls to the work they do and the relation of that work to the work of others in the building up of industrial and other systems. As we have already seen the Call to salvation must issue in some sense of mission, and lead us to treat our job, whatever it may be, as one element contributing to a common good, Providence is concerned not merely with persons, but with things and the relations of persons to one another and to things. We may think of this as a pyramid of vocations,[1] as a hierarchy of vocation-values,[2] or as a cosmos of callings, it makes little difference, so long as we recognize in it the divine plan for the world. Our Christian faith is that there is, or should be, a calling in which everyone's particular gifts of ability and grace can find full occupation and fulfilment.[3] Humbly and prayerfully, as we seek to choose our life's work, and at each crisis, where fresh choices are put before us, we must seek God's guidance where to go and what to do. He is interested in those things and has a purpose for our lives, if we are willing to be guided by Him in obedience and devotion. On the other hand, the man whose motive is ambition, in its obvious form of *hubris*, or in the more subtly disguised forms which ambition can readily assume, seeks and will only accept the kind of job that keeps himself continually in the middle of the picture, where God ought to be, and tries to arrange the cosmos round his personality and its ambitions—such a man cannot escape from distortion, "*Angst*", "eccentricity", frustration and insecurity, and must be in a continual ferment of assertion, claim and counter-claim, adventuring far

---

[1] J. A. Robertson, *Divine Vocation in Human Life*, pp. 152-66.
[2] Ritschl, *Justification and Reconciliation*, pp. 44-66.
[3] See, on this, Part II, Chap. 16.

beyond the boundaries of his own talents and normal opportunities. His personal relationships will reflect the distortion of his business activities and he will contribute directly to the restlessness which robs modern man of his serenity and prevents others from finding and fulfilling their vocation.[1] For the Church there is the corresponding ideal of the Body of Christ, within which there is great diversity of organ and of function, and in which each should find his place and opportunity in accordance with his *charisma*. "The work we do for a living is only one part of our vocation."[2] The Church is not perfectly the Body of Christ, any more than the world is a perfect cosmos of callings, but these conceptions are no *mere* ideals, wishful thinking, but the real plan and purpose of God for each and all. In finding his place in the Body of Christ, a man will also find the point where he can witness to the Gospel in the world in which he lives, for every member of the Body of Christ is meant to be an active agent of His mind and will in the world. "Fain would I be to the Eternal Goodness what his own right hand is to a man." Ambition is too squalid a word to describe an aspiration so noble and a devotion so awe-inspiring.

There have been many attempts to classify "vocations", by Ritschl among others, none of them wholly satisfactory, for the same reason as makes casuistical classification of virtues and codification of duties so unsatisfactory. We have seen cause to reject Brunner's contention when, following Luther, he maintains that the housemaid and the artist are on a level so far as their actual occupations are concerned. "The valuation of work is shifted from the 'what' to the 'why' and 'how'."[3] Brunner does not make clear how far he accepts Luther's dangerous but necessary distinction between the "Christian" and the "secular" station—the vertical and horizontal "dimensions" of vocation—and so his conclusion

---

[1] V. A. Demant, *Religion and the Decline of Capitalism*, *passim*.
[2] Reeves and Drewett, *What is Christian Education?*, p. 14.
[3] Brunner, *Christianity and Civilization*, II, p. 62.

seems more equalitarian than Luther would allow, though he himself is no equalitarian.[1] There *is* something intrinsically more noble about "Johann Sebastian Bach composing a cantata in honour of God" than about Johannes and Uli watching a calving cow, and meanwhile enjoying fraternal Christian conversation,[2] though it would be as difficult to assess the respective spiritual values as it would the market values in each case. Johannes might get more for his calf than Bach for his cantata!

Nor is it possible to compare the spiritual value of certain vocations in accordance with the amount of sacrifice they involve. "Don't send us", said James Chalmers of New Guinea, "men who talk of self-sacrifice." "He was right," says Bishop R. O. Hall: "the missionary's job is the happiest in the world. But you have to pay for happiness. . . . Being a missionary is like being married. Your happiness and your joy are in other persons' lives."[3]

Here we find again that the vocation-value of any calling is to be measured by the way in which it furthers personal relationships and satisfies human needs, not merely in extent, but in the dimension of depth. Here again, we see why and how the ministry is, or ought to be, the vocation of vocations, the calling of "the parson". All its material media are, or should become, symbolic of personal relationships.

If this "vocational" attitude to life has any validity, the vocation of each must have reference to "my station and its duties". Indeed this phrase is simply the inadequate ethical description of the doctrine of the calling without taking its distinctively religious character into account. Strictly speaking, this sense of vocation, of treating my work as a calling, can only be *a response to a call* and bears a close relation to the experience of forgiveness, as Ritschl and Brunner point out. Strictly speaking, therefore, a "secular vocation" is a contradiction in set terms, unless it means, as it should mean, the

[1] *Ibid.*, p. 67.
[2] *Ibid.*, p. 63.   [3] Quoted by Norman Blow, *Christian Vocation*, p. 41.

Call to serve God in the various "secular" spheres. The old antithesis between sacred and secular, important though it must remain, is no longer a relation of mutual exclusiveness and antipathy. This calling is both an individual and a universal thing, it is unique and at the same time representative of the whole of reality. The whole world finds its focus for me in my calling.[1] The forgiven sinner can never attempt to group or construct his world round himself as the natural man tries to do. Once he reaches and recognizes the place that God means him to fill, everything in his life assumes its proper dimensions and falls into its proper place. He is no longer governed by his own self-interest or vanity, but by his response in faith and obedience to the Call of God.

In this way, as Brunner points out,[2] the Christian is saved from the dilemma of renunciation of the world, or compromise with it. He acknowledges that in his calling he may and must act with a clear conscience, though his conduct may be far from perfection in the abstract, ethical sense. He cannot accept "the relativities of history" as if they were final, nor remain inactive till ideal conditions present themselves.[3] Still less does he lie awake at night lamenting his lot in this imperfect world. In all his behaviour he must remember that to be a Christian means to accept a vocation and treat all his life as a calling, turning his necessity to glorious gain.

The ministry is the vocation of vocations, not because of any sacerdotal privilege, but because it is the representative calling, the minister is "the parson", set apart from the market-place to be the unique and representative person, to

[1] *The Divine Imperative*, p. 212.
[2] See J. A. Robertson, *op. cit.*, pp. 148 ff., and Ritschl, *op. cit.*, pp. 445-52. Note in Ritschl particularly the contrasting of the ethical and distinctively theological aspects of vocation, and the close relationship of the vocation of Jesus to the vocation of the Christian.
[3] "We do not find absolute situations in history" (K. Mannheim, *Ideology and Utopia*, p. 83). But paradoxically enough, Mannheim goes on to maintain that we can have "paradigmatic experiences" in history that have revealing significance beyond history and therefore may be claimed to have absolute validity (*Diagnosis of Our Time*, pp. 131 ff.).

minister to the elect, and to demonstrate in one person the unity of all three meanings of vocation, election, mission and the dedication of daily life. He is the minister of the Gospel.

This principle of vocation properly understood then is the great motive which drives men to work without allowing them to believe that either they or their fellows are mere hands and feet or brains. They are personalities with souls, and their association should be the free society of responsible persons in which they toil for the Glory of God and the welfare of their fellow men. These are not two ideals, but one. The Glory of God and the true interest of my neighbour coincide when a man recognizes and fulfils his calling. They both coincide also with his own true spiritual welfare. "Let thy work appear unto thy servants, and thy glory unto their children. And let the beauty of the Lord our God be upon us, and establish thou, the work of our hands upon us: yea, the work of our hands establish thou it". (Ps. 90: 16, 17) He finds himself and discovers his liberty in willing service and obedience. In such toil, fulfilling a calling, his work has significance and purpose, and therefore in it, however monotonous drudgery it may seem, is joy. The noblest aspiration any man can have, in the ministry or anywhere else, is to "walk worthy of the vocation wherewith we are called" (Eph. 4: 1). To those who do so, St. Paul, in the most admirable Manual for Ministers ever written, namely 2 Corinthians, promises: "We all with open face beholding as in a glass the Glory of the Lord, are changed into the same image, from glory to glory, even as by the Spirit of the Lord" (2 Corinthians 3:18).

Chapter Sixteen

VOCATION, PERSONALITY AND FELLOWSHIP

In recent decades Christians have largely subscribed and pandered to popular illusions about the idea of "vocation". "Each man has his own vocation," said Emerson. "The talent is the call". A man's vocation or a child's vocation was taken to be the occupation in which he could best express himself, for which he was best fitted, from which he would derive most pleasure and satisfaction. There is a great deal of romanticism and, in fact, nonsense in the notion that all men and women should be able to find a job in which they will be able perfectly to express themselves, and that if only careers masters, appointment boards, and vocational psychologists are given free course everyone will be able to find his ideal niche in the social scene.

Certainly it is a good thing that boys and girls should, so far as is possible, be guided to the jobs for which they are best fitted, among the limited range of jobs that will be open to them. But it is folly to encourage the idea that they will all be able to find complete satisfaction in earthly occupations. The business of keeping this world going always has involved a vast amount of drudgery; it does so at present, and it is always likely to do so. There is an element of drudgery in the most interesting jobs. The most satisfying jobs are in the end unsatisfying. Christian teaching should not conceal this hard and prosaic fact. It has no need to do so, since it does not pretend that the fulfilment of man's destiny lies in this world or in his earthly occupations.

A man's earthly calling is the task appointed by God in which he is to obey Him and serve his brethren. This calling reaches a man normally through the operation of natural causes. For the great majority of mankind the earthly calling is determined within narrow limits by the place and time in which they are born, by heredity and environment, and by the opportunities which the state of society provides. Boys born in mining villages are generally called to be miners, the sons of farmers to be farmers, and so forth; and the exceptions prove the rule.

It is perhaps a misfortune that most of those who write and talk about this subject are themselves exceptions to the rule, and that they are generously inclined to suppose that the comparatively free choice of an occupation which has been possible for them is a universal possibility. This generous impulse blinds them to the fact that the idea of a man's vocation to his earthly work—an idea which is hardly explicit in the Bible, so far as individuals are concerned—does not supersede or abolish the obligation of mankind to do all the ordinary, humdrum jobs that are necessary to maintain the life of the world. A man finds his vocation in doing as well and as cheerfully as he can that part in maintaining the life of the world which is assigned to him, and his assignment is determined within narrow limits by circumstances which he cannot control but which he can accept in terms of his responsibility to God and the neighbour. It is obvious that the life of the world could not go on if every man was at liberty to choose precisely the job which appealed to him most, yet this has been the logical conclusion of the modern romanticism about vocation. Theologians will be doing a useful piece of work if they call this particular piece of bluff.[1]

Nothing more true or more necessary has been said recently on the subject of vocation than these wise words of Dr. Alec Vidler. But the Reformers would applaud every word. They were under no delusions as to the grim necessities of life, and they never offered their disciples self-realization in the eudaemonist sense, any more than our Lord Himself did. A headmaster, recently rebelling against the glib use of the words "a sense of vocation", declared that a sense of humour was far more important for a teacher! It is important that all those concerned with the "vocational" guidance and training of the young should be brought to realize that there is much more in the idea of vocation, both

[1] *Theology*, Nov., 1949, pp. 401, 402.

psychologically and theologically, than the fitting together of a kind of jigsaw puzzle of people and places, care being taken as far as possible, to keep square pegs out of round holes and vice versa. We have no intention of decrying the value of the technical aspects of vocational guidance, of discovering aptitudes and training them into skills, but the weakness of this whole approach is its ignorance of or indifference to the ends to be served and consequent inability to deal with the various motives involved, as witness the present pathetic attempts to discover "adequate incentives".

As has been said, in many cases "work is still done just because it needs to be done",[1] but men will not go on doing it indefinitely and unquestioningly unless they believe it is worth while in some sense, either spiritually or materially or both. Ultimately it must prove itself worth while in both senses, spiritually important and materially effective, or it will not continue to provide an "adequate incentive".

There are many motives to work, of varying degrees of urgency and ethical importance. A surprising number of men work because they like it, because they would rather be busy than idle. Most men work because they have to; some for love of money; some with an artist's or craftsman's interest in exercising skill in creating things that are the best of their kind or aesthetically satisfying. Some are chiefly moved by the desire for power or for privilege of some kind or public esteem, by a desire to escape from mediocrity, by a sense of duty, a desire to benefit other people, or by a religious sense of vocation because they feel called to work to the Glory of God.

It is unlikely that any of those motives ever operates in its purity. Man is an amphibious animal and his action is usually due to a complex combination of pushes (economic and other pressures) and pulls (spiritual ideals). Even the artist who lovingly creates his masterpiece, has to live, and

[1] Demant, *The Listener*, June 22, 1950, p. 1078.

probably to bargain for its price.[1] Anyone who regrets the necessity of assessing art in terms of the market-place must remember how many masterpieces have been wrung out of great artists by disagreeable and inexorable necessities. (For example, Beethoven and his nephew, Handel, Oliver Goldsmith, etc.) Very few artists have been such shrewd business men as Anthony Trollope, whose literary production worked with the deadly precision of a taximeter.[2] Even in the case of the ministry, where men are supposed to be immune from the concerns of the market-place, men must live and married men must support their wives and bring up families, and money worries may stultify a promising ministry. On the other hand in coping with such worries a true minister may learn how to preach to those similarly beset, who will probably be the majority of his congregation. Complete emancipation from such cares would probably lead him to occupy a pulpit in Cloud Cuckoo Land.

It is the contention of this book that none of these motives, apart from religion, nor any possible combination of them without religion, is a sufficient and satisfactory motive for work, because of man's nature, his status in the sight of God, the character of the world in which he must live, and the purpose of God in setting him "in his calling".

We must not imagine that the distinctively religious sense of vocation is something which must supersede all other motives, or can be added to them. It must dedicate and so transform them. Perhaps certain motives such as love of money cannot be so dedicated, as the Early Church found was the case with the master-slave relationship. The Apostle Paul was not a Pharisee plus a new interest; the whole focus and purpose of his life was changed. The religious motive of a sense of vocation works upon the raw material of secular circumstances and the character of the agent. The subsequent behaviour is not a creation *ex nihilo*.

[1] See Benvenuto Cellini's *Memoirs, passim.*
[2] See *An Autobiography, passim.*

But when we invoke religion we must remember the innumerable cases in history where the entry of religion has made a problem completely insoluble, and transformed motives which till then were more or less reasonable into fanaticisms which are quite implacable. How often the statesman and the educationalist try to "keep religion out of it", because, to their minds, religion is essentially sectarian, imports strife into a situation instead of providing a principle of synthesis, and turns factors, which were capable of integration into some sort of community purpose, into demonic idolatries.

Religion will not provide our souls and our societies with a principle of synthesis on the superficial level of an occasional "church parade" as an instrument of promoting morale. In the last resort it is Amos and not Amaziah who contributes more to the upbuilding of Israel. Prophetic religion is no more convenient or amenable socially to-day than it has ever been, but in the long run it was the message of the prophets with all its rigours and explosive violence and not the Temple ritual that held the Jews together throughout their miraculous history. So it is not the slightly sanctified or enlightened self-interest, beloved of the politician, that really contributes most to human welfare, but the complete surrender of the soul to God without counting the cost, as we see it in St. Francis and beyond all comparison in our Lord, that really overcomes the world and transforms all our values, and builds Jerusalem in every land.

This is not romanticism in Vidler's sense, or idealism in the Marxist sense, but plain prophetic realism, trying to look at the facts of life in all their crudity, yet with prophetic vision of the mind and purpose of God at work in human history. Neither human aptitudes nor human circumstances are made of cast-iron. The thing that makes a vocational ethic so difficult, is that man is no longer confronted with a nature more or less inhospitable to spiritual purposes, but yet bound to yield and become serviceable if dealt with by skill and devotion. In a sense that battle with nature has been won, though hard experience is teaching us that even nature cannot be exploited with impunity, but must be approached reverently and handled lovingly. Dustbowls and groundnuts are hard teachers of grim lessons. The god in the machine has his limitations. But our worst predicament at present is the spiders' webs of human contrivances that make so many men feel their only rôle is that of the fly. You can't talk to a fly in a spider's web about Providence and vocation.

A real sense of vocation would radically transform most of our circumstances by relating them to standards, and translating them into terms of service to God.

> All service ranks the same with God:
> If now, as formerly He trod
> Paradise, His presence fills
> Our earth, each only as God wills
> Can work—God's puppets, best and worst,
> Are we; there is no last nor first.
>
> Say not "a small event"! Why "small"?
> Costs it more pain that this, ye call
> A "great event", should come to pass,
> Than that? Untwine me from the mass
> Of deeds which make up life, one deed
> Power shall fall short in, or exceed![1]

So Pippa resolves that she will envy nobody,

> Being just as great, no doubt,
> Useful to men and dear to God, as they!

We find the prototype of this simplicity and sense of values and of the significance of little things, in our Lord Himself. But Pippa goes on from her springtime rapture:

> God's in his heaven—
> All's right with the world!

to the grim necessities of daily life:

> Tomorrow I must be Pippa who winds silk,
> The whole year round, to earn just bread and milk.

[1] Robert Browning, *Pippa Passes*.

Religion is no mere holiday fancy, when people may escape at springtime and find in nature what they lack in daily life and work in a town. That would be a recrudescence of the belief in *banausia*, consigning the "dark Satanic mills" beyond redemption. The spiders, the "men of destiny", weave the web, the flies are caught and sucked dry. It is possible so to believe in religion and even so to teach it to the young, as to render men docile under injustice, and to dope them till they are equally insensible to the realities and the possibilities of life. Equally it is possible so to represent the need for perseverance in Grace and for serving God in our calling as to create a spirit of ruthless exploitation under the guise of religion. But neither of these can any longer claim to be true teaching on vocation, as we find it in Scripture and in the Reformers.

It is not enough that those who have the vocational guidance of the young should have a smattering of psychology, considerable technical skill and a fairly extensive knowledge of the tendencies of the labour market. It is important that what men and women do in life should bear some reasonable relationship to what they are: it is even more important that they should have insight into what they are in the sight of God; and should choose and accept their work in life, its stern necessities as well as its opportunities, and in fact learn to see the opportunities in the necessities, and find freedom in accepting responsibilities.

What expert in vocational guidance would ever send Albert Schweitzer to Lambarene? On all grounds of economics, psychology and philosophy, such a choice involves almost criminal waste of brilliant talent, amounting to genius, in music and theology, squandered in providing elementary medical help to a depraved tribe in West Africa. But on religious grounds of vocation this heroism provides a magnificent example of true vocation, which has inspired multitudes to sacrifice and dedication.

It is almost inevitable that unless Church and State somehow co-operate in framing the new social patterns of the future the whole apparatus of government may be employed to promote "welfare", construed in purely material terms, to provide "vocational" guidance and training on a basis of market values and technological demands, leading the young to choose their "careers" and prepare for them with little idea of social service and much thought of material gain, till our whole culture and its civilization are poisoned and perverted even more than they are at present by a money mentality.

On the other hand, it is no longer possible, fortunately, in politics, in industry, or in education, to impose religious "tests" upon all those called to leadership. It is all the more important that the truly religious standards and values in our Christian tradition should be recognized and maintained, that agreement on certain basic values, without which, as Professor Demant has reminded us, even *laissez-faire* could never have functioned, should require "a minimum conscious conformity of behaviour" in the rulers, and a certain ingrained but "largely unconscious behaviour" in the community they rule, though from neither rulers nor ruled can we expect explicit belief such as is expected within a Church. While we vehemently disagree with the first part of the quotation, a part of T. S. Eliot's *The Idea of a Christian Society* (pp. 26–28) is too pertinent to be omitted.

Even if, in the present conditions, *all* persons in positions of the highest authority were devout and orthodox Christians, we should not expect to see very much difference in the conduct of affairs. The Christian and the unbeliever do not, and cannot, behave very differently in the exercise of office; for it is the general ethos of the people they have to govern, not their own piety, that determines the behaviour of politicians. One may even accept F. S. Oliver's affirmation—following Buelow, following Disraeli—that real statesmen are inspired by nothing else than their instinct for power and their love of country. It is not primarily the Christianity of the statesmen that matters, but their being confined, by the temper and traditions of the people which they rule, to a Christian framework within which to realize their ambitions and advance the prosperity and prestige of their country. They may frequently perform un-Christian acts; they must never attempt to defend their actions on un-Christian principles. . . . I should not expect the rulers of a Christian State to be philosophers, or to be able to keep before their minds at every moment of decision the maxim that the life of virtue is the purpose of human society—*virtuosa . . . vita est congregationis humanae finis*; but they would neither be self-educated, nor have been submitted in their youth merely to that system of miscellaneous or specialised instruction which passes for education: they would have received a Christian education. The purpose of a Christian education would not be merely to make men and women pious Christians: a system which aimed too rigidly at this end alone would become only obscurantist. A Christian education would primarily train people to be able to think in Christian categories, though it could not compel belief and would not impose the necessity for insincere profession of belief. What the rulers believed, would be less important than the beliefs to which they would be obliged to conform. And a skeptical or indifferent statesman, working within a Christian frame, might be more effective than a devout Christian statesman obliged to conform to a secular frame. For he would be required to design his policy for the government of a Christian Society.

We have to postpone for future studies detailed examination of the comparative vocation-values of different trades and professions, particularly as these might be put before children by those responsible for their training and their choice of a "career". A girl who appears to have ability sufficient to justify her advisers in persuading her to train as a teacher is offered a post as a prospective saleswoman in a shop. How are the respective merits of the two "careers" to be put before her? Prestige favours the teacher, glamour and immediate pay the job in the shop. Salesmanship contributes to the community, so does education. Each has its *banausia*, its opportunities of advancement, holidays, etc. Each requires and develops certain gifts. We have already seen how all-important it is that those who teach must have a sense of vocation.[1] Yet girls have confessed that they thought of teaching only when they realized they could not succeed in any more exciting job. How far has the picture-house put glamour and money in the forefront of children's lives, so that they come to think of these as the only things that matter?

A boy whose father owns a pottery wants to be a poet. Is he to be encouraged to refuse to enter the family business and devote himself to the muse? Or to attempt to bring poetry into the pottery as genius has been able to do before? A butcher's son wants to be a surgeon! . . .

Inasmuch as vocation is of its very nature individual, and to each individual his own vocation is peculiar, the guiding of men towards the discovery of their vocations is a task for the evangelist and pastor rather than for the philosopher. But the discussion of the general conditions to be fulfilled may be undertaken by the philosophy of religion or natural theology, and the implications of the actual occurrence of vocation can hardly be ignored. It is evident that the whole doctrine of Providence is involved. For the divine will or purpose, which determines my vocation, also determines all events or occurrences whatsoever, at least in the sense of fixing the order within which they take place. It must therefore be possible in principle for a man to discover his vocation by considering with sufficient thoroughness his own nature and his circumstances. In practice, however, to achieve the necessary degree of thoroughness is often so difficult as fairly to be called impossible; where all possible effort has been made to ascertain by such means the direction of vocation, it is sometimes at least found by a conscious communion of the mind with God. Such guidance by an Inner Light is an experience common among those who make a serious practice of religion in any of its higher forms, and in some of these, as, for example, among Christians in the Society of Friends, it becomes the dominant element of a great tradition. But it is not only so that vocation is discovered; it may also be found by the ordinary exercise of a mind which has in prayer committed itself to the divine guidance. That vocation exists, and where experienced provides the practical solution of the main ethical problems, is the clear testimony of religious history.[2]

[1] See above, pp. 183–4.   [2] W. Temple, *Nature, Man and God*, pp. 407, 408.

It is unlikely that more than a minority will ever treat the choice of a life-work on this high level of consecration. But, to revert to T. S. Eliot's argument, even if only a minority do so, they may create such a pattern of behaviour that others in their multitude may come to share in some sense the experience of living within a providential order, and so escape the cosmic loneliness of lost souls without roots in tradition or fruits in purposeful lives. As we have tried to show, such a belief, even if unconscious, has nothing enervating about it, but has the utmost positive value in promoting a sense of security within which faith may proceed to adventure with some degree of confidence. And besides those who listen for the Call of God upon their knees there will be many who are saved from false choices and guided into serviceable paths, because they have been brought up to see more in life than money or glamour or power. The Church has to-day a duty and a vocation so to present the Christian faith in market-place and school that even when the response of full belief and commitment in discipleship does not follow, recognition of the Christian values may be inculcated and Christian patterns of life be built up.

While most hymn books include Cecil Frances Alexander's beautiful hymn: "All things bright and beautiful"; most modern editions omit the original third verse:

> The rich man in his castle,
> The poor man at his gate,
> God made them, high or lowly,
> And ordered their estate.

Compare with this fatalist and quietist teaching the much older hymn with its admirable teaching:

> Teach me, my God and King,
> In all things Thee to see;
> And what I do in anything,
> To do it as for Thee!

A man that looks on glass,
On it may stay his eye;
Or if he pleaseth, through it pass,
And then the heaven espy.

All may of Thee partake;
Nothing can be so mean,
Which with this tincture, "for Thy sake",
Will not grow bright and clean.

A servant with this clause
Makes drudgery divine:
Who sweeps a room, as for Thy laws,
Makes that and the action fine.

This is the famous stone
That turneth all to gold;
For that which God doth touch and own
Cannot for less be told.

GEORGE HERBERT

In the one we are taught to conform to inexorable circumstances, in the other we are enabled to transform all circumstances by a transfiguring sense of vocation by God.

Index

A. PERSONS AND BOOKS

Dorner, I. A., 59
Duncan, George S., 30

Ecclesiasticus (Jesus ben Sirach), 131
Einstein, Albert, 7
Eliot, T. S., 103, 107, 113, 114, 211–12, 214
Emerson, R. W., 204
Encyclicals, *Quadragesimo Anno*, 175, 192
  Rerum Novarum, 192
Encyclopaedia of Religion and Ethics (E.R.E.), 52, 75
Ephesians, Epistle to the, 138
Epictetus, 40
Eusebius, 42–3, 44, 45, 51, 137

Fanfani, F., 49, 152–60, 163, 164
Fergusson, Bernard, 20
Figgis, J. N., 98, 157
Flew, R. Newton, 47–8, 151
Fowler, W. Warde, 123, 127, 128
Fox, George, 99, 196
Francis, St., of Assisi, 50, 85, 90, 144, 145, 208
Frederick the Great, 88
Freud, Sigmund, 7, 8, 63, 82, 85
Fromm, Erich, 98
Fuggers, The, 160
Fuller, Bishop, 16

Gandhi, Mahatma, 76
Genesis, The Book of, 23, 128–31, 177, 188
Georgics (Vergil), 122
Gladstone, William Ewart, 82
Goldsmith, Oliver, 207
Gordon, General, 86
Grant, General, 24
Green, T. H., 58

Hall, Bishop R. O., 201
Handel, G. F., 207
Hannay, Canon J. O., 52
Hartmann, von, 58
Harvard Report: *Education in a Free Society*, 17, 20
Hastings: *Dictionary of the Apostolic Church* (H.D.A.C.), 75
Herbert, George, 214–15
Herodotus, 28, 126
Hesiod, 121, 122, 129, 131, 136
Hildebrand, 109

Hitler, Adolf, 9, 25, 87, 90, 107, 171
Holl, Karl, 153, 154
Hügel, Baron von, 72
Huxley, Aldous, 159
Huxley, Julian, 114
International Review of Missions (I.R.M.), 82, 92
Isaiah, 28, 109

Jehovah, 26, 27, 29, 34
Jenkins, D. T., 183
Jerome, J. K., 116
Jesus, 29 *et passim*

Kammerer, Otto, 185
Kant, Immanuel, 52, 62, 63
Kierkegaard, 83
Kirk, Bishop K. E., 35, 40, 49, 50, 143
Knox, John, 69, 150
Koestler, Arthur, 178–9, 186

Lactantius, 74
Lambeth Report, 11
Lang, Archbishop Cosmo Gordon, 89–90
Lemoine, 159
Lenin, 9
Lightfoot, Bishop, 41
Lincoln, Abraham, 24
Lindsay, Lord, 26, 53
Livingstone, David, 82, 85, 86, 91
Livy, 127
Lockhart, J. G., 89–90
London, Bishop of, 139
Lord, A. R., 69
Lucretius, 122
Luther, 51, 53, 59–61, 85, 147–51, 154–67, 169, 173, 200, 201

Macgregor, W. M., 15, 26, 197
Machiavelli, 163, 169
Mannheim, Karl, 63, 114, 202
Manson, T. W., 30
Maritain, Jacques, 152
Marryat, Captain, 196
Marx, Karl, 7, 8, 63, 64, 95, 153, 162, 173, 176, 180
Matheson, J. G., 148
Meecham, Henry B., 41, 42
Micah, 90
Moberly, Sir Walter, 82
Moffatt, James, 75
Moody, D. L., 82

218

B. SUBJECTS

Absolute Ethic, the, 44, 49, 74, 79
Absolutism, Kantian, 64, 65
Accidie, 142
Aesthetic, 135
Agapé, 85
Ambition, 82–94, 157, 201
Amtsperson, 150
Ancient world, the, 54, 55
Angst, 170, 199
Apocalyptic, 100
Art, and work, 117–19, 123, 124, 169
Artisans, 126, 127
Athens, 121, 123
Atonement, the, 136
Avocation, 15, 16, 35

Banausia, 124, 132, 134, 142, 210
Barthian(ism), 99, 103
Behaviourism, 102
Benedictines, the, 143
Beruf, 154
Biology, 7
Body of Christ, the, 34, 42, 105
Bourgeois ideology, 173
Britain, 11, 171
Buddhism, 82
Burning Bush, the, 28
Byzantinism, 188

Calling(s), the, 17 and *passim*
Calvinist—Puritan, 137
Capitalism, 152–67
  and industrialism, 160–64
Career, 16, 17
Casuistry, Protestant, 161
Catholic ethic and bourgeois mentality, 160
Catholicism, Roman, 50, 96, 97, 153–67
  of despair, 10, 170
Celibacy, 45, 78
Charisma, 196, 200
Charity, 72
Child-birth, as punishment, 129
China, 108
Chosen People, the, 22–9
Christian patterns, 214
Christianity, 26, 44, 95, 116
Christians, as the soul of the world, 41

Christendom, 93, 114, 194
Church, the, *passim*
  and State, 192, etc.
  Anglican, 99, 108
  Confessional, 194
  Early, 54, 55, 74, 188, 207
  Methodist, 106, 108
  Orthodox, 20, 187, 192, 194
  Presbyterian, 108, 194
  Protestant, 20, 80, 192, 194, etc.
  Roman, 20, 50, 65, 80, 96, 97, 99, 192, 194
Cistercians, 143
City of God, the, 21
Civilization, 83, 100, 108
  European, 114
  Greek, 123
Clergy, secular and regular, 143
Collective security, 75
Communism, 97, 98, 108, 109, 113–14, 115, 172, 174, 186, 189
Conatus in suo esse perseverare, 166
Conscience, 57–66, 71–2, 93
Contemplation, 126
Conversion, 88–9
  of St. Paul, 33
  of Archbishop Lang, 89–90
Corinthians, 126
"Cosmos of Callings", 21, 105, 186, 199
Counsels of perfection, 38, 52
Covenant, the, 22–9, 33, 57
Craftsman, 118
Creation, 21, 128–31
Crisis, morality of, 38
Cross, the, 21, 30, 31, 57, 78, 84, 86
Crusade, a, 69
Culture, negative, 113
  gentleman, 116, 122
"Curdling" of the Christian Ethic, 45–7

Denominationalism, 104–10
Destiny, 82–94, 105
Dialectic materialism, 174
Disestablishment, 96
Divorce, 38
Doctor, Vocation of a, 182
Drudgery, 204